Cyber Economics

Digital resources are changing the world

ANTÓNIO BELO SANTOS

This first edition was first published in February of 2018

Editor:
Fountain Intermediation Services S.à.R.L.
7, rue Robert Stümper, L-2557 Luxembourg
T: (+352) 26 73 02 1, F: (+352) 26 73 02 20

ISBN: 978-1-7320625-0-4 (Paperback).
ISBN: 978-1-7320625-1-1 (EBook).

20 19 18 / 3 2 1

DEDICATION

This book is dedicated to Vera and Leonor, with eternal love and gratitude.

CONTENTS

ACKNOWLEDGMENTS

This book took two years to research and mature. To be totally fair, I wasn´t even thinking about writing it at all.

But sometime in earlier 2018 my Guardian Angel whispered in my ear that the time had come to share the information contained herein with the world.

As years go by I have been trying to listen and act upon the wise whispers of my Guidance, for which I am so eternally grateful, and that is the reason why I wrote the book.

Writing is a joyful activity and writing this book was a

pleasure, but I would not have done it without loving support.

My wife Vera has assisted me tremendously. Words fail as I try to verbalize my gratitude to Vera's caring love.

May Vera be showered with many blessings of love and light.

The fullness of love, which is the Truth of the universe, cannot be described into words, nor can it ever be digitized, it can only be felt and experienced in all its glory.

António Belo Santos

Lisbon, Portugal

February 2018

PREFACE

The world is rapidly becoming a better place. We all know it; we all feel it. Our complex daily life is certainly facilitated by the widespread adoption of digital resources, which enable us to do more, reach further, be more effective and become more creative.

The companies we manage, and the industries we operate in, will inevitably go through a period of digital transformation. Over the coming years, new ways of running the same businesses will be found and, as always, new businesses will emerge to seize the many opportunities coming up every day.

That is all perfectly fine, but of course our role as

business leaders is to understand the strategic implications of digital transformation, lead the way forward and implement our vision for the future of our businesses and their contribution to the communities we support through our activities.

Societies at large, and our businesses in particular, rely on our sound judgment about which are the most beneficial, efficient ways to adopt digital resources and rely on our ability to make choices that are in the best interest of all.

Therefore, as we take deliberate steps to execute business strategy for the companies we oversee, the question in our minds will sooner or later necessarily be how to calibrate the speed and intensity of digital transformation in the pursuit of corporate strategy.

As always, too much or too little will not work very well, - we are seeking the right amount of digital transformation, at the right pace, at the right time. Embracing the digital transformation too fast and too furiously can look good on paper, but may not make economic sense and could disrupt our Clients and our organization; but proceeding too slowly or without adequate intensity may erode our competitive position over time. Easy to say, harder to accomplish, this is.

Therefore, as business leaders, many of the choices we face today rely on our ability to correctly assess the depth, breadth, speed and measurable impact of the adoption of digital resources.

Towards that end, three main questions require straight answers:

- Could it be that digital technology is a mere optimization and simplification tool utilized by society with the aim of assisting us in doing the same things we did before in an easier, more efficient way?

- Could something more strategically relevant than mere optimization emanate from the adoption of digital technology that requires deeper consideration in the way it will impact the way the whole economy works?

- Could the digital revolution produce consequences that reach so far and wide into the fabric of society that it completely reshapes human interaction on a global scale?

These are three very complex questions of critical relevance to the calibration of investment and management choices that will impact our organizations and society in a significant way.

Let us take this opportunity, while focusing on an economic perspective, to search for useful answers by observing what is happening all around us.

INTRODUCTION

This business strategy book delivers a fresh perspective of the dynamics of digital transformation.

Written for professionals and focusing on the global business leader's perspective, this book identifies and reviews the most powerful dynamics generating key strategic consequences for businesses today as a consequence of the generalized adoption of digital resources by society as a whole.

Focusing on the dynamics of Cyber Economics for the business strategist, the book reviews critical strategy developments emerging from digital transformation in agriculture, artificial intelligence, blockchain technology, cyber security, education, fashion, Fintech and banking, health and wellness, insurance, marketing and the consumer, real estate, transportation and smart cities, tourism and hospitality.

Adopting a keenly direct approach and using concise, straight forward language, the book aims to contribute towards a holistic perspective of the dynamics currently operating in the marketplace as a consequence of widespread digital transformation.

Throughout the book we deliberately avoid discussing often-biased academic perspectives and the relatively few quantitative scientific studies available in the field, instead focusing on identifying the core Cyber Economics dynamics and strategy at play in each of the themes.

Business leaders active in each field can then complement the concepts discussed in the book with their own research based on effective industry and company data as they prepare specific strategies applicable to their case.

As a means to assure the fluidity of the discourse, and considering that this is a book written for professionals, we will assume that the reader is comfortable with business strategy and general management concepts and is able to immediately elaborate from those.

We will start our journey by exploring what digital resources are and seek to further our understanding of the root causes that support their widespread adoption as convenient means to manage information.

In our next step we will look at some of the cross-industry impacts of the widespread adoption of the dynamics of Cyber Economics as we look to understand the reach of the digital transformation process.

Our work will then address the most fundamental risks involved in the adoption of digital resources and outline key antidotes to manage these risks.

Then we will move on to observe effective implications of Cyber Economics in today's business world. We will broadly address the present state of play of adoption of digital technologies across several industries, outline the strategic choices being made to face the challenges presented and focus on specific areas of business that will likely be more impacted by the continuous adoption of digital resources.

By publishing this business strategy book, we ultimately hope to contribute towards the formulation of a clear view of what Cyber Economics really is and its ability to directly impact our world and our investment choices as business leaders.

WHY DIGITAL RESOURCES ARE SO USEFUL

This may come as a shock to you, so let's start by putting it front and center – digital resources are limited, but that is exactly what makes them so useful.

The world seen through a digital interface looks fundamentally different from the aworld experience that we are used to enjoy as humans.

In the world we all live in as humans, the potential of experience is unlimited, everything is connected with everything else at all levels, and the possible interactions are limitless.

The reality that we experience as human beings is composed of infinite subtleties and complexities, which make our world so much richer than any other form of expression that we are consciously aware of.

Think about the difference between a photograph and the physical presence of the person. Regardless of how incredibly high the definition of the photograph is, it will always pale when compared with physical presence, which is so much more contextual and has so much more information and potential.

Have you ever preferred to have a face-to-face meeting instead of a videoconference? These are completely different experiences. There is simply so much more wealth in personal interaction that you cannot compare both ways to conduct a meeting, and this illustrates how different digital resources are when compared to the wealth of our human experience.

As we go about our daily lives, we are literally swimming in an ocean of infinite possibility, and that is really something to feel grateful for, because there is nothing that comes even close to it.

Think about all the options readily available to you at this very moment, even if for simple things, such as how you will decide to spend your day today. The potential ahead of you is endless at this very instant. For all you know, suddenly something, anything really, could happen that completely changes everything for you and for many others around you. The possibilities of what can unfold at any given moment in our analogue reality are truly unlimited.

And of course we are all familiar with popular stories of people who change the direction of their lives simply by deciding not to pursue a certain career, or even take a certain bus back home, or start a fortunate or unfortunate new relationship; and how much that seemingly simple decision potentially impacts, not only individual lives, but potentially even the entire world.

The infinite possibility we constantly experience in our world in each given moment is yet another evidence that the truth of our universe is abundance - not just abundance of resources or material goods, or even creativity or ingenuity, rather the unlimited abundance of possible expressions of truth and unlimited perceptions and interpretations of such truth.

Moreover, not only your options in the world of human experience are unlimited but we also live in a world where everything is interdependent.

Any subtle changes in any little point of the reality we live in can impact so many unpredictable things and generate unforeseen outcomes with tremendous repercussion.

But it turns out that all this incredible wealth of possibility and interaction, which characterizes the world we live in, can be incredibly complex too.

Complexity is by its very nature hard to harness and manage. Quite simply, there are so many variables at stake in everything, everywhere, at all times, that there is no way that we can be absolutely certain of all the consequences of each of our choices.

As a business leader you know from hard experience that you cannot predict with certainty what will happen when you roll out your next business initiative simply because the interactions it will create are endless.

And if you even try to dominate and control your business rather than just seeking to influence it, significant uncertainty and inefficiency will emerge of your attempts.

Think about all the time, energy and resources humanity has spent while trying to produce controllable outcomes in rich complex contexts and the phenomenal cost and inefficiency we have had to deal with while struggling to do so.

Throughout history, human societies have sought to find ways to prosper without falling prey to cornucopia of complexity. Many people asked themselves the same question – what if we could find a simple way to help us deal with the complexities of life that would also allow us to interact with each other and support each other?

But then, one day, really dumb machines came around and we started trying to explain our complex, rich world to them, to make them helpful. That was the moment when the world started changing and digital transformation began.

It was only when we were faced with the dilemma of trying to explain our incredibly rich reality to really dumb machines that we devised the simplest strategy we could come up with – digital technology.

Digital technology describes reality as a set of 1´s and 0´s and it completely disregards all other possibilities that are in between of these absolute "On" or "Off" attributes.

When stripped down to their core, all digital resources are no more than a vast collection of 0´s and 1´s, combined in very long strings of information. Throughout these long strings of information, there is no in between. There is no distortion, no potential, no limitless possibility and no subtlety. Quite the opposite, in the digital world, reality is described as either a 1, or a 0, and that's it.

Therefore, digital resources are able to capture only a limited perspective of reality. Call it a slice of life, if you want. That is exactly why digital resources are so incredibly useful. The slice of life that digital resources capture is so much simpler than life itself that it can be tremendously useful.

It is exactly because digital resources are inherently limited and artificial – digital resources are unable to describe reality in its fullness – that they are so much easier to control and manage than reality itself.

The apparent weakness of digital resources therefore has one single attribute that we can harness to our benefit – simplicity that can be managed.

The inherently simplistic digital resources offer invaluable assistance to us and ultimately serve as fundamental means of unleashing our creativity and effectiveness.

Reality as described through a digital interface becomes lighter, clearer, simpler and easier to manage. Digital resources offer no room for interpretation – it is all black or white, yes or no, on or off.

The exact moment when we realized just how helpful it would be to use a simplistic way to deal with reality is the moment when digital transformation became inevitable.

Having the possibility to control even a slice of

reality, instead of not being able to control anything at all, is so tremendously helpful to the advancement of society and of course to everyday business that it will forever change our world for the better and incredibly speed up humanity´s evolution.

Besides simplicity, another fundamental benefit we can draw from digital resources to our business life is that it sets a common frame of reference – a unique language if you will - that we can use globally for collaboration and coordination purposes, which of course is empowering in unimaginable ways.

Through the adoption of the dynamics of Cyber Economics, as we embrace digital transformation, we became able to gradually establish a simple, common framework that can be universally used to describe reality through standardized programming methods.

We can instruct machines to operate under the same rules and the communicate with each other, thereby establishing an eco-system with a sufficient level of harmonization that ultimately allows an unlimited number of machines to connect and share information at global level in real time.

When business leaders understood the power of creating eco-systems of machines, which can collect information, combine it and share it with other machines, humanity started evolving on the path of digitization, as we all started converting parts of our rich reality – capturing slices of life – into digital format, where these become information that can be put to positive use.

Those were the first steps of data collection and early digitization, during which we started creating data that represented our reality, storing this data in machines, instructing the machines to make connections between the collected data and with other machines and starting to apply this newly found wealth of data to solving concrete everyday situations.

And then we started connecting larger and larger number of machines together over large networks where the digitized data was shared and we found that, once formerly isolated machines are interconnected and instructed to start working together, they operate as if they are one larger machine of industrial size and capacity.

This means that from operating isolated machines in our factories we moved on to embrace a new paradigm when we created what effectively is one single global industrial machine through the interconnection of an enormous swarm of individual machines which all collect, store, combine and share digital information.

That is how the dynamics of Cyber Economics and digital transformation entered the global stage.

For the first time in history, computer networks where billions of machines articulated under the same set of rules are creating what can be best described as a one global industrial machine that is put to universal service and is potentially used by each and every person on the planet.

As the new industrial machine composed of all the machines interconnected grew bigger, we saw how to strategically deploy digital technology with newly created industrial capacity to economic objectives, and that is the moment when Cyber Economics was born.

Therefore, Cyber Economics refers to the ability that large industrial scale machine networks have to act collaboratively and impact the way we do business, effectively generating specific dynamics that transform our economies through the widespread adoption of digital resources.

Cyber Economics can be seen as describing a new phase of industrial revolution in the sense that the dynamics and the consequences of generalized digital transformation are profound and tremendously beneficial to society.

The unleashing of a worldwide, pervasive, universal

industrial machine is incredibly empowering to the masses and will bring about a new universal economic paradigm, a new economic deal to which we will refer to as Cyber Economics.

For the more sceptical, as always, the immediate question is "Qui Bono"? i.e., who will benefit most from Cyber Economics?

Even tough Cyber Economics was not established for altruistic reasons or even for humanitarian reasons, the unintended consequence of the mass adoption of digital resources and the emergence of Cyber Economics is that the public in general is the entity that will benefit the most from it.

Not only does Cyber Economics represent the creation of the largest industrial endeavour humanity has ever taken, it also grants the general public direct access and interaction with it.

The benefits at an individual, group and societal level

emerging from Cyber Economics are massive, universal and have profound worldwide implications impacting the future of humanity.

For the public in general, the first and foremost consequence of the emergence of Cyber Economics as a new global economic deal is the unleashing of an unprecedented wave of freedom and independence.

Through the adoption of the dynamics of Cyber Economics, many people will be able to solve problems in ways they never thought possible, for the first time introducing the notion that independence and entrepreneurship of the individual are supported by humanity as a whole and by the participation in specific groups that the person freely chooses to associate with.

Independence means not being dependent on others. In that sense, Cyber Economics is empowering to individuals and communities, as they become able to unleash their creativity and problem solving capability, enabling individuals to operate independently while being supported by humanity as a whole in their personal efforts.

The Dynamics of Cyber Economics is inherently supportive of personal freedom and entrepreneurship.

Digitally transformed businesses create the unprecedented opportunity for large numbers of people to conquer personal freedom from the bondage of employment and debt as a consequence of being able to invest in their own skills and their own personal brands.

The use of digital resources can be highly liberating and release humanity from many forms of slavery, such as for example by eliminating the need of the individual to succumb to burdening job relations, instead being able to operate freely in marketing their unique skills across global markets.

Many elements of human interaction will be up for review as a consequence of the adoption of the dynamics of Cyber Economics and many of the existing outdated economic structures will be profoundly transformed.

Anything from relationships to deals to ways of doing business will be subject to assessment and will ultimately be cut off if there is a better way.

And of course because access to the new industrial machine is permanent, and universal, Cyber Economics enables change to occur at the fastest speed possible, completely breaking away with the previous rhythm.

Inventions like the kitchen stove, the radio, the refrigerator and even electric power took decades to reach the majority of the world population as the adoption of new technologies took many years to become effective and have an impact in society.

But digital resources are being impacted at speeds previously unheard of. Smart phones, social media, tablets and Internet access took years, not decades, to become available to the wide majority of the world population.

The main explanation for the staggering pick-up in speed of adoption of new technologies is the wide availability of these resources to the general public and the network effect emerging from the online collaboration of large parts of humanity.

The staggering speed at which the world economy is moving into a Cyber Economics is unheard of in human history and will surprise any of those who disregard the sheer power of the transformations that the way we relate and do business with each other are going through.

In that sense, Cyber Economics will ultimately become a big awakener. It will present humanity with totally unexpected challenges, but it will also provide the instruments for radical, collaborative new solutions and scientific discoveries to be brought forward to deal with these challenges.

And that is the reason why business leaders are being called upon to effectively oversee the implementation of the most adequate strategies to empower companies to thrive in the new context of Cyber Economics.

BORDERLESS WORLD

The massive, fast adoption of digital resources by the business community is benefic to society and is one of the main benefits of Cyber Economics.

But the inevitable interconnectedness that the dynamics of Cyber Economics establish at a global level requires business leaders to look at their businesses with global perspectives that often can be challenging to the company's status quo.

Let's review some of the key ways in which a genuinely global approach to business will impact the way business leaders outline and implement corporate strategy.

The first and foremost change in perspective for business leaders that emerges from the borderless world established by reliance on digital resources is the requirement to understand that they are managing one company, regardless of borders.

Companies that operate on a local level and have yet to fully embrace the digital transformation have a tendency to become attached to "the way things have always been done around here" and many other "home office syndromes".

Do not bee fooled to think that this narrow business perspective only happens to small mum and pop businesses. Quite on the contrary, it seems. Many companies that grew very large in their historical home markets over many decades are the ones facing the deepest, hardest challenges.

When large local companies start their so called

"internationalization process" by establishing an "overseas business division", this is inevitably a recipe for disaster in the digital world.

The disaster emanates from two very simple observations: (i) the cosy decision of establishing an "overseas business division" implies that the company continues operating in business as usual mode in the local market, while trying to copy and paste that very same model to other markets, and (ii) that the company headquarters will actually put an effort to distance itself from what happens "overseas", with the effect of focusing more on financial statements and profitability of "overseas operations" and less in taking advantage of the learning curve that exposure to several markets brings.

One could even think that business leaders who manage their cross-border businesses with such an "overseas" approach think of themselves as the emperors of the Roman empire when they assume that whatever happens across the empire outside

Rome is left to be managed by the generals posted there, and all that matters is the cash flows that can be extracted from the provinces. This is an absolute disgrace.

In the current world there is only one company, regardless of how large it is and regardless of weather it uses legal subsidiaries for legal and operational reasons across different markets. It doesn't matter - in the end, the company remains one single company.

And for this company to be able to operate across borders, business leaders must embrace digital transformation in such a way as to allow the company to approach the business with a global view.

A business leader who embraces Cyber Economics seeks to accomplish a profound internal transformation that allows the company to operate successfully independently of geography. That is why the "overseas business division" is absolute nonsense in the digital world – the entire company should function harmoniously across borders, based on the adoption of digital resources.

The second change in perspective for business leaders that emerges from the borderless world established by reliance on digital resources is that the ultimate ruler of everything is the Client.

Business leaders with a universal perspective know that their business strategy needs to be grounded somewhere, and that is no longer geography, but rather it is the Client.

And of course this implies that, given the global reach that Cyber Economics brings to the business, fame and fortune come to those who are willing to adapt to the specific needs of Clients across many geographies, resisting the urge to treat them all disregarding their specific desires, preferences, local characteristics.

The third change in perspective for business leaders that emerges from the borderless world established by reliance on digital resources is the absolute focus on the values of freedom, independence and change.

Yes, this company started in certain geography, but it may well happen that the local market has become stagnant and mature and it may well be that growth opportunities arise throughout the world.

Business leaders focusing on establishing business strategies for their companies must approach choices with the notion that the company is free to move anywhere, establish itself anywhere, build infrastructure anywhere, and that change will bring the company to a new level of independence, profitability and resilience.

Establishing a corporate business strategy that puts the company's growth, freedom and independence first can be dubbed as an unconventional approach first, but a few years down the line it will be seen as the only rational approach and in many cases the only way to escape stagnant growth and profitability.

Independence means not depending on others, i.e.,

not being required to abide to the so called authority of others who are only protecting their petty personal interest and do not keep the company's best interest at heart.

In that sense, the adoption of digital resources to transform a local company in an inherently international company means questioning "the way we do business around here", moving in a different direction than the one portrayed by the status quo, acting in unexpected ways, unyielding to negative established in-house corporate interests.

That is why business leaders in the Cyber Economics world must be independent and should not come from the ranks. Quite on the contrary, they should be perceived as rebels, restless original thinkers and planners to whom nothing else will do until the company becomes truly global.

The fourth change in perspective for business leaders that emerges from the borderless world established by reliance on digital resources is the understanding that the power of the business leader is directly impacted by the adoption of digital resources.

People used to say that it could be lonely at the top, because often business leaders have found themselves inadvertently shielded from much information that could assist them in the formulation of corporate strategy.

Many people in organizations are delighted to offer immediate solutions to business problems that inevitably spring up every day, or even worse cover them up as long as they possibly can, but this often occurs at the cost of the root cause of these problems not even being identified, much less addressed, often with disastrous consequences.

Digital resources, combined with AI, are tremendously empowering to business leaders not only because these resources unearth issues to where they can be faced, but also because at corporate level these resources are ultimately at the disposal of the business leader, even tough they are often deployed across a multitude of geographies.

In that sense, the adoption of digital resources can be liberating to the business leader, in the sense that cuts off blockages that would often delay or even block access to vital understanding of what is going on in the company.

The fifth change in perspective for business leaders that emerges from the borderless world established by reliance on digital resources pertains to the backgrounds of management and the consequences to their thought process.

Companies which operate only on their local market and have yet to embrace digital transformation tend to hire local managers, who mostly share the same cultural, educational background, and therefore share fundamentally similar perspectives of the world and tend to focus on the comforts of the home market.

As the adoption of digital resources unleashes the dynamics of Cyber Economics in a company and it is transformed into a global player, management teams become gradually more diverse.

Management diversity is always a sign of different perspectives being applied to management issues, but it also raises the bar on the quality of the decisions being adopted simply because there is less ability to cope with local based perspectives.

This wider approach to decision making which emanates from diverse management teams therefore inevitably makes the decision process more analytical and more based on the data provided by digital resources and AI, and in those cases home country perspectives gradually lose weight in the decision making process.

The above mentioned changes in perspective that business leaders experience through the adoption of digital resources, when combined, are a signal of professionally humble approach of the business leader to the problem solving process, which is one of the hallmarks of powerful leaders and an effective predictor of stellar outcomes.

CREATIVITY

Business leaders who embrace digital transformation as part of their strategic vision for their companies seek to internally enhance creativity across the organizations they lead.

But how exactly can digital resources assist in making a company more creative?

By themselves, machines are unable to be creative, even if powered by AI. This is because machines rely on past data to function; they are unable to extrapolate without referring to a previous data set that can be used as a frame of reference.

Digital resources cannot dream, machines cannot imagine, computers cannot grasp the subtleties of context and therefore they are unable to create something that is unique and original, to which meaning can be attributed.

But the nature of digital resources is such that business leaders can be put these to use in meaningful ways to empower the entire organization become more creative.

Digital resources liberate humans from repetitive, unrewarding tasks, freeing up time and predisposition for more creative endeavours. The deployment of digital resources across organizations implies a thorough overhaul of the job functions in the entire company, substituting non-creative activities with more contextual, creative, problem solving functions.

Then, as the organization becomes more advanced, business leaders expect people to collaborate with each other relying on assistance by digital resources. In that context, human collaboration is accelerated across the company through the use of several information sharing and communication technologies supported by digital resources.

Additionally, the support offered by data analytics to the most productive, innovative ideas significantly contributes to assure that helpful advances are conceived, empowered faster and sooner than before. One of the key competitive advantages of companies who embrace digital transformation is the added capability to quickly reject inefficient ideas, projects, and ways of doing business, while supporting valid creative advancements to the way the company operates or the products and services it offers.

As the company reaches out into the world, digital resources play a significant role in breaking down many of the existing barriers previously existing between the company and it's Clients and other stakeholders, with numerous benefits.

When business leaders steer their companies towards creativity, thereby turning them into creative companies, opportunities start freely manifesting themselves for the company to effectively support Clients in their own creative process.

In the world of Cyber Economics, fostering individual creativity has become a global, fast growing business. The use of digital resources and digital platforms can provide a wealth of inspiration to assist creative in becoming creative, and in that sense they are a fundamental invention that will leverage the advancement of society.

As the global population interacts freely through digital platforms, countless new ways of being inspired become up each day. Our human imagination is stimulated like never before through all the information and ideas being shared across digital networks at any given moment. Business leaders who understand how deeply valuable to society the facilitation of creativity really is are able to strategically align their companies to become part of the on-going explosion of creativity by allowing their companies to support the creative energy of society as a whole.

Another consequence of adopting digital resources and fostering internal and external creativity is that companies who promote creativity become more risk propense.

Solving problems in creative ways implies taking chances through trial and error while trying different approaches to previously unsolved problems. Creativity emerges from the human ability to jump into the water, not knowing how to swim, and then see what works, while of course incurring in the risk of drowning.

The creative process implies not following a linear process and instead leaping over the previous inappropriate solution to find another way to solve an old problem.

This ability to deal with risk and accept it as a part of life, even when efforts fail and unhelpful consequences emerge, is a fundamental element of the culture of successful companies. Business leaders to promote creative companies and invest in fostering the opportunities where the companies they manage offer support to the creativity of others are promoting a culture of risk tolerance that is a fundamental pillar of success.

Finally, business leaders who unleash the creative potential in an organization create a less stressful environment for people to work at, which in turn transpires into a more relaxed relation between the company and the external world.

Creative Business Leaders are keenly aware that the creative process requires stress free environments and periods of time during which you are not even trying to be creative are fundamental to effectively speed up the creative process. These apparently slower periods of time are absolutely essential for creative solutions to emerge. But then, when ideas come up, digital resources can incredibly speed up the testing, validation and implementation of ideas in such a way that makes the production of the positive outcome of the entire creative process strikingly fast and efficient.

In this sense, digital resources are creativity enablers by fostering happier work places, promoting great internal and external relationships, and contributing to empower business leaders to transform the companies they lead and society as a whole in meaningful, fresh ways.

CYBER TRUST AND SECURITY

Cyber security is the protection of information systems, the data they store and the services they provide from unauthorized access, damage or misuse by authorized system operators or by unauthorized third parties.

As companies from all sectors embrace digital transformation and benefit from the dynamics of Cyber Economics, their exposure to the serious risks posed by digital networks becomes elevated.

In today's world, significant numbers of daily cyber

attacks and attempts to exploit any weaknesses in digital resources are increasingly frequent, specifically target successful businesses and high new worth individuals, assume elevated levels of sophistication and can have devastating effects when successful.

The survival, continuity and prosperity of companies rely heavily on the ability that business leaders will have to effectively attribute an elevated role to cyber security in company strategy thereby promoting the safeguard of technology, data and networks from a multitude of threats.

The market and regulatory pressure exerted over companies to take cyber security very seriously is paramount as a consequence of the personal nature of the information that companies are now collecting about people and their lives.

The risk of any security breach can therefore cause immediate deep financial and reputational damage through the theft or compromise of sensitive data and intellectual property, hurt the company's reputation and challenge it's competitive edge.

The main problem with cyber security is that, in the fast moving digital environment, security measures that work today will quickly become obsolete making the company become at peril of breach in a very short period of time. And so, to put it mildly, let's just say that a company's security will always be work in progress.

So let's discuss some of the most basic immediate steps that business leaders can take to tackle the strategic challenge posed by cyber security.

The first, most important step is to elevate cyber security to a high priority status in corporate strategy, which will of course have ramifications across all of the company's activities.

In doing so, business leaders are focusing on identifying the risks that the company is incurring while facing information security challenges and will then move on to enhancing the management of digital resources.

In thoughtfully prioritizing cyber security, by acting very realistically about the company's effective ability or inability to protect and defend it´s digital resources, the wide majority of business leaders will seek external support and procure the most qualified external cyber security professional services available.

In the case of companies active in certain sensitive areas or companies which have a larger impact in society, business leaders will most likely seek to approach and partner with government institutions in the context of enhancing the company's cyber security measures. And in the case of small companies or companies that do not have so relevant roles in society, business leaders look for industry associations that can often provide shared services to several companies acting in the same field. Regardless of the specific circumstances of each company, with very few exceptions, business leaders will seek assistance from specialists in their efforts to promote cyber security, and will not face the challenge alone.

The next logical step is to undertake a company wide assessment of stress points and fragilities and address these openly through the adoption of a cyber security governance plan, which contemplates adequate investment in digital resources and software and empowers all levels of the organization through access to effective tools and training.

In the course of implementing a cyber security strategic plan, companies seek to identify which groups could become potential offenders and review appropriate measures to adopt in order to pre-emptively limit their ability to effectively do harm.

A wide array of potential offenders should be considered, depending on the relevance that a company has in society and the business area it is active in. Potential security offenders can conceivably extend from highly sophisticated state sponsored actors to isolated individuals.

State sponsored hackers seek to obtain political, diplomatic, technological, commercial or strategic advantage, focusing mostly on government, defense, finance, energy and telecom sectors.

Companies acting in certain areas of the economy that attract media attention for dealing with large numbers of people or serving the public in general are also at risk of suffering hacking actions originating in terrorist groups.

Another source of concern can originate from hacktivist groups who act illegally in response to certain social or political issues.

“Script Kiddies”, mostly individuals who use hacking software made by others, are also a concern especially for companies that process reasonably high levels of financial information from their Clients, such as credit card numbers that can then be sold in illegal websites on the Internet.

And finally trusted insiders, even at elevated levels of responsibility, should be considered as a potentially serious cyber security threat as a consequence of their free access to critical systems and data in the company. Trusted insiders can be current or former employees of the company and also its external providers who interact with digital resources with certain level of privileged access. It could conceivably occur that certain insiders maliciously facilitate external attacks targeting digital resources or that they compromise key data for their personal benefit. It could also occur that benevolent insiders inadvertently compromise the company's systems through negligence or simple lack of understanding of the full consequences of their actions as they exercise their privileged access to sensitive systems and data.

Once cyber security implementation measures are in place, business leaders seek to constantly reassess the adequacy of the company's approach to cyber security challenges and update the corporate cyber security plan accordingly.

Cyber security is one area of significant concern in a context of Cyber Economics and a challenge to digital transformation of companies and societies as a whole.

But the fact that we are faced with a challenge only means that we put it front and center in our field of vision, deal with it adequately and continue moving forward.

There is much more complexity involved in cyber security than we can ever address in a business strategy book, and what is even worse is that all of it will be outdated very soon, so let's not waste our time.

The key observation of relevance regarding cyber security in the context of a business strategy book has already been made clear but we will make it even clearer – for the wide majority of companies, trying to manage Cyber Security alone based only on in-house talent and resources is senseless.

Cyber security is a topic of extreme relevance for the survival of companies. It should be highly prioritized in the company's strategy and subject to frequent follow up and review. The smart approach to deal with cyber security is to hire the best professional specialists you can find, empower them, and make the technological investments required.

Team up with the specialists and take a conservative approach because it is tough out there, and it will get much tougher before society as a whole is able to put in place the infrastructure required to assure private companies and individuals better defenses from cyber security challenges.

ETHICS

Successful business leaders are passionately committed to truth. They realize that truth is the ultimate competitive edge in business, as in life, and that most of the leadership work they deliver is devoted to aligning the companies they oversee with truth.

Imagine you have been appointed to the job of CEO of a large company and consequently are experiencing an inflated ego for being "the chosen one to lead the way".

After you stop massaging your ego and get back to earth, you may be in for the rude awakening that occurs when you find that the company is facing intense issues and a wide array of challenges that will require extreme efforts and flexibility to deal with.

Feeling like a "superstar", you may come in with a plan that you have imagined to solve it all, but somehow the "difficult" people working in the company or the "imposing" Clients just do not seem to get along with what you have in mind.

The worst part of the entire ordeal of course is that there is really no escape from that burdening job after having taken the seat, which means that it could all become so less glamorous and appealing in the end than what you anticipated or had been led to believe initially. This happens every day, and many business leaders will only privately admit to this reality.

But are there any secrets to deal with the challenges posed by the many veils that separate you from the truth?

Of course there are, and they emanate from business ethics.

One of the strategies that effective business leaders use to overcome their egos and see the truth is taking deliberate steps in the exact opposite direction of what their egos are telling them to do.

This is akin to saying that one of the secrets behind inspiring leadership is to consciously choose to take a professionally humble approach to whatever challenge is being presented.

Professional humbleness is about reducing the tone of the permanent chatter in your mind, lower the tone of your voice, actively listen and become a receiving antenna to what the universe is trying to tell you, sometimes even bluntly in your face, instead of childishly trying to implement some solution that is yet another brainchild of your ego. This is of course an ethical way of approaching business.

That is the moment when answers start becoming apparent and solutions, regardless of how difficult, emerge and a way forward is carved. That is the real moment of truth.

Another strategy to success that business leaders are well familiar with in their efforts to be aligned with the truth is to always inspire, support and uplift others and make sure that the corporate strategy is committed to these values. Business ethics is rooted on the notion that you build what you stand for.

A third strategy that business leaders implement as they align with the truth is to quietly observe what the company has less resistance in doing, what comes natural to the company culture and is an inherent uniqueness that can be put to use if focused in the right direction. And of course natural law and natural cycles are fundamental elements of business ethics.

As business leaders start walking the path of alignment with truth and fostering an ethical way to approach business, success is increasingly more effortless, inevitable and overwhelming, simply because all success in life comes from truth.

And the best part of it all is that there is no competition to the level of success that can be achieved as a consequence of pursuing truth, because there is no opposing counterforce to it.

But exactly why are we going through these more philosophical notions and ethics consideration in a business strategy book focused on Cyber Economics?

Because it turns out that digital resources are unable to recognize truth from falsehood, and that is a dangerous double-edged sword. By themselves, digital resources cannot determine what an ethical approach to business is and therefore these resources can be used effectively to pursue both ethical and unethical approaches.

As an example, you can assign an enormous database

full of false, blatantly inaccurate data to a cutting edge AI enabled machine and it will not be able to tell if the data is true of false. Much worse even, if so directed, the machine will then treat the data as the only existing reality, analyse the false data and suggest next steps according to the analysis it made using the data, which will inevitably lead to disastrous consequences.

Digital blindness to truth is a direct consequence of the limited nature of digital resources – they are completely unable to assess the quality of the data at their disposal.

Consequently, business leaders have the absolute responsibility to adopt and inspire ethical behaviors while overseeing the strategic management of digital resources, effectively directing the use of machines for the greater good, avoiding any possibility that these resources can eventually be used to be deployed against truth.

This is why business ethics are so very important to

business leaders while overseeing the deployment of digital resources in the context of Cyber Economics.

So how can business leaders inspire ethical business practices in the management of digital resources through their actions and their decisions?

The first, most powerful approach that business leaders adopt towards inspiring ethical business practices is being trustworthy and expecting equal behavior form others.

As leaders, we educate others through our own examples. We strengthen in the organizations we oversee the identical elements that reflect our core values. When we support trust through our actions, life trusts us in return.

Trustworthy business leaders generate powerful waves of confidence, which extend to the entire organization they are overseeing and also extend across its boundaries.

The second powerful approach that business leaders adopt towards inspiring ethical business practices is recognizing that success cannot be achieved by striving to get it. Instead, success and achievement emerge as a consequence of what we truly are. Success is a reflection of virtue, not a virtue itself.

The same happens with companies – they become successful by being the best at what they do. Great companies are in a league of their own, they really do not have peers; rather they redefine the businesses they operate in, leading where others follow. Success happens when companies focus on excelling at what they do best as a supporting pillar of a community. Super successful companies appear to have a certain coolness, a special vibe to them and can even operate in discrete and unassuming ways, simply because the entire company knows how to truthfully deliver on its promise and is fully committed to doing so.

The third, approach that business leaders adopt towards inspiring ethical business practices is effectively getting rid of bad actors and unethically minded people, regardless of how technically expert they are or how apparently irreplaceable they might be. If the actions of someone working for the company you are overseeing demonstrate that they are unable to trust or be trustworthy only on the basis of their spoken word, send them away as fast as you can. And while you are doing it, use the purging momentum to get rid of people who are uncaring, cynical and are always seeking to get something in return in the way they approach others. This will impact the company's culture significantly and effectively promote business ethics to a pillar of your strategic plan.

By the way, this extends not only to every bad actor in the company, but also to unethical suppliers and unethical Clients. Push them out and let them be an evidence of what is not acceptable. If unethical Clients are constantly draining your resources by being overtly demanding beyond the realm of the service they are purchasing from you, get rid of them.

You can, and should, fire your unethical Clients. And if you ultimately cannot get rid of a Client, then tell them that you will service them at no cost until they go away because this will gradually diffuse their hostility towards the company and eventually they will leave.

The fourth, most powerful approach that business leaders adopt towards inspiring ethical business practices is by growing out of bad business ways of doing business.

Towards that end, business leaders simply explain to others that "the way the company did things in the past does not cut it anymore" and so the company is moving on to a much healthier way of doing business.

And how does this apply to Cyber Economics and management of digital resources?

The key focus of business ethics in the digital world is how data is handled.

Companies operating to high ethical standards in Cyber Economics actively seek to only collect, store and process data through digital resources that is strictly needed to execute their tasks and do so with the express informed consent of the Client. In one word, you can summarize it all by saying that ethical companies deal with digital resources with restraint.

Think of data as both an asset and a liability – you want to have a controlled approach to it following strict, auditable proceedings and guidelines.

The purpose of the company you are overseeing is not to transform you into the new ruler of the world. That is a megalomania that only works in children cartoons and fiction books.

Keep in mind that the world is becoming a better place. Societies are becoming more resilient. And as liberty and freedom are expanded through the deepening of Cyber Economics, societies become more and more resistant to any dictatorial urges, regardless of how sophisticated. In fact, the purpose of your company is to serve and support society and lead by example and what this means is that, in what regards to data, you act carefully and thoughtfully.

Ethical businesses operating in Cyber Economics do not indulge in data mining practices just because they can. They do not spy on their Clients, they do not collect and do not process data without the Client effectively understanding why the data is being collected, what the purpose of the data collection and treatment really is, and has provided clear authorization towards that end.

Once having adequately and lawfully collected, processed and stored data, ethical businesses active in Cyber Economics deploy all their best efforts to protect the integrity of the data from any harm, thereby defending the privacy of the Client, which implies refraining from sharing Client data in any form, unless that is specifically required by the Client for a particular purpose related with the rendering of a specific service.

Towards that end, ethical businesses active in Cyber Economics are stringently demanding with their own staff in all that pertains their digital behaviour, which includes the enforcement of rigorous internal controls and guidelines regarding who has the right to access data and how that person is required to interact with the data.

By doing so, ethical businesses active in Cyber Economics earn the trust, respect, investment and business volume that make them successful in what they do as a consequence of what they are and what they stand for.

Knowing your Client is one thing – spying on your Client is another.

Business leaders are therefore called upon to assist the strategic establishment of digital citizenship, acting by example through their influence in the companies they oversee and in the communities they support.

Ultimately, the adoption of business ethics enhances Cyber Economics and empowers business leaders to understand that the opportunity to inspire ethical behaviour is contributing to the establishing of a free world where respect, transparency and truth are the basis for economic and social development.

COMPLIANCE

Insert In Cyber Economics, compliance is the name of the game.

As the dynamics of Cyber Economics accelerate and digital resources amplify the consequences of inappropriate actions, societies are vigorously demanding an increasing oversight of all digital activity and placing added weight in the value of digital security.

Many business leaders have been vocal of the fact that digital transformation is generating a global quest for compliance, law, order, transparency and accountability, and this trend is likely to continue and accelerate as the digital transformation of society deepens.

Not surprisingly, legislators and government officials are responding to society's push for data security by enacting new, more stringent regulations and by increasing control and enforcement measures.

Regulators are assisted in their efforts by the fact that enforcement of appropriate conduct in the digital world is facilitated by the permanence of data.

Once data is created it simply does not go away, it does not disappear, which makes it much harder for untrustworthy agents to cover up their actions and more likely that law enforcement officials are able to correctly identify and punish offenders.

Consequently, in the near future business leaders managing digital transformation will be expected to continuously expand the role of compliance in the organizations they oversee and actively develop partnership relationships with regulators with the aim of facilitating the evolution process inside the company.

Over time, the dynamics and speed of Cyber Economics will evolve significantly and become so pervasive that even the best, most well funded and staffed regulators will be unable to effectively control everything that is going on in all corners of the digital space.

The next step emerging from Cyber Economics will then be the gradual decentralization and automation of compliance.

In digitally mature environments, the community will quickly identify noncompliant behaviour, flag and expose it and immediately react to it by reducing the level of trust granted to the untrustworthy agent.

Compliance and control functions will be assisted by

digital resources, which will independently conduct many compliance surveillance activities on a continuous basis.

The gradual decentralization and automation of compliance will have the effect of largely reducing non-compliance.

Working together, organizations and regulators with effectively promote the spotting of inappropriate behavior in early stages, before it can place large parts of society at risk.

And finally, decentralized automated compliance will change the way retribution for noncompliant behavior is delivered.

Less people will serve jail time – putting people away and forgetting about them is not the most sophisticated way of dealing with inappropriate conduct.

Instead, ill-thought trust-compromising actions will

be publicly registered and amplified; consequently people who adopt these non-compliant actions will be less trusted by the community, which will in turn significantly limit their opportunities and make their life significantly more difficult and expensive and ultimately less rewarding in all regards.

As a consequence of remaining visible to all after having been proven unworthy of trust, people who incur in non-compliant actions will be required to put in an additional effort to re-conquer the trust of the community and that effort alone will be a signal to society as a whole of the real value of trust.

In this context, decentralized, automated compliance will ultimately reduce the overall cost that society will have to incur to assure the compliance function, while effectively signaling risks and promoting compliant behavior.

Business leaders overseeing companies active in Cyber Economics master the art of embedding self-regulation into the strategic alignment of the organizations they oversee.

By demonstrating through their actions that compliance leadership is a key competitive advantage in Cyber Economics, business leaders influence organizations towards the adoption of compliance as a business strategy is by itself an effective differentiator in a digitally transformed world where reputation and trust are fundamental business attractors.

PLATFORMS

Everybody seems to be talking about the "sharing economy" – so let´s have a look and see what this is all about.

When referring to the notion of "sharing economy", people seem to be addressing the use of digital platforms to connect supply and demand in areas of the economy where the piled up excess capacity creates an opportunity to explore significant efficiency gains.

In consumer based economies, large value items

which represent significant investments are frequently purchased by end Clients and subsequently generate zero income while being subject to effective utilization patterns that extract only a small percentage of the entire capacity of the asset, effectively rendering these purchases a pure misallocation of resources.

Some examples of this reality are second homes, yachts and cars, and in general anything that owners do not put to use most of the time.

Any business leader you talk with will tell you that depreciation and maintenance cost without any return, in a context of low utilization is the definition of misallocation of resources.

What this misallocation of resources does to the owner´s portfolio is pure raw damage as these emotional expenditures, which cannot really be seen as investments, carry the cost of significant value destruction.

Consumers who were left stranded with a fast depreciating and little used asset in their hands after having completed significant, mostly unused purchases, were unable to find alternative use for their assets and consequently saw the part of their wealth invested in them evaporate.

If you take a broader view and consider the issue from the point of view of society as a whole, the sheer volume of waste in value and resources involved in high investment but low utilization purchases is staggering.

Furthermore, from the perspective of the economy as whole, widespread misallocation of resources effectively diverts investment away from financing economically productive activities and increases the cost of living as a consequence of the need for individuals to outright purchase assets that they could otherwise use on a need to do it basis.

Being cognizant of this reality, for many years

marketers have directed enormous investments to the ethically questionable purpose of associating the purchase of certain types of goods and services with emotional attachments in the mind of the consumer, seeking to establish ego based justifications to economically unjustifiable expenditures.

The reason why this was tolerated was the relatively high barrier to entry that the cost of marketing these assets for partial use would represent, and the absence of trust in the entire process of marketing unused resources, both from asset owners and from those who would eventually be interested in partial use arrangements. The entire process was inconvenient and ineffective for all involved.

As people tried to navigate around this reality, the mitigation strategy most people used often relied in mid-term arrangements, especially in real estate, but these were insufficiently agile. Other strategies revolved around the use of intermediaries and brokers who, more often than not, simply added noise, complexity and cost to potential transactions.

But the adoption of the inherent dynamics of Cyber Economics completely changed the game.

As interconnected digital resources started reaching a wider base of the world's population, Cyber Economics enabling platforms started offering the public in general an effective means to address the issue of marketability of misused assets.

What these multiple platforms have in common clearly illustrates the dynamics of Cyber Economics.

On the supply side, Cyber Economics enabling platforms reduce barriers to entry by lowering or effectively erasing the cost of listing an asset in real time, whilst providing a certain level of marketing and communication that asset owners themselves would be unable to justify from a pure cost to income standpoint. These platforms also add value to the asset owner by enhancing trust in the transaction through the collection of some level of information about the Client, which is much better than the total absence of information previously experienced. Moreover, the review system offered by these platforms empowers asset owners who focus on providing stellar services to stand out from the crowd and market their offers on the basis of trust in a very efficient way.

On the demand side, Cyber Economics enabling platforms offer the convenience of choice, the added trust emanating from the identification of the provider and the reviews offered by the community; but above all these platforms offer the public in general a new level of convenience and flexibility, whilst promoting the gradual reduction of costs.

While some consumers could suffer from a marketing induced emotional attachment with assets like cars; when the financial advisor comes into the room many will consider not owning a car at all and instead use a digital platform based service to assure their transportation needs and many others still will even consider becoming the drivers in such a service to handsomely supplement income and find a productive use for their free time and improve the capacity utilization of their car.

The consequence of the widespread adoption of Cyber Economics enabling platforms is phenomenal.

The first fundamental change is that assets previously left unused suddenly become available for short-term utilization, which of course generates a significant impact for the owner who previously had an all-cost and zero-income situation. As the asset's capacity becomes gradually occupied, suddenly the asset becomes cheaper to own, run and depreciate, and the owner's expenditure starts operating more like an investment and less like an emotional purchase. Hence, the owner´s cost-base is reduced without really losing any of the ability that the owner keeps to still enjoy the asset for personal purposes whenever desired. The second fundamental change is that consumers who would never be able to purchase a certain asset, suddenly have the ability to use it much like they owned it, while disbursing only a small fraction of the price.

These changes are inherently deflationary as they significantly reduce costs for supply and demand and represent significant gains in efficiency for society as a whole.

Think of all the cars, yachts, homes etc. that will no longer have to be built whilst at the same time all the ones who were built are used to higher levels of capacity.

And then consider the emerging consequences for society as a whole and for the environment emanating from the improved allocation of the freed-up resources.

Over time, society will discover that the dynamics of Cyber Economics apply not just to cars and homes, but effectively extends to a wide array of products and services which can go from cleaning services, to professional services, to credit finance, to office space and even private jets – any resource that can be put to use in a more efficient way.

As the use of Cyber Economics enabling platforms becomes widespread, the combined effect in the mind of the consumer is to become less emotionally attached to specific objects.

Ownership will be less valued than the ability to experiment, as people become more focused on their ability to access and use resources for their desired purposes.

Business leaders adopting the dynamics of Cyber Economics will prioritize business strategies that offer usability as the key benefit, and ownership as a mere alternative.

The implications in the shift in perception in the mind of the consumer about how to best utilize assets will significantly impact marketing strategies.

Marketing of usability will continue to be rooted on emotions, but will shift away from ownership and focus on use.

In turn, ownership of resources will gradually make more sense to people and companies who specialize in owning and managing certain classes of assets and are willing to use parts of their professional time in maximizing capacity.

Ultimately, as a direct consequence of the adoption of digital resources to overcome market inefficiencies, the standard of living will improve for the public in general as a consequence of wide-spread adoption of the dynamics of Cyber Economics, while both trust and reputation will emerge as fundamental differentiators in the marketplace for both businesses and individuals.

SKILL FORCE

As more companies embrace the dynamics of Cyber Economics, business leaders are overseeing a profound transformation in the way all kinds of work is effectively accomplished.

In a Cyber Economics context, digital resources and AI effectively execute a wide array of functions, while humans assume new and much more rewarding roles of complex, technical and creative nature, most often integrating specialized teams operating through professional networks.

In this context, business leaders are placing their strategic focus on the specific skills that each team member is required to have in order to be able to integrate advanced interdisciplinary teams, coordinate technically complex matters, and help find creative solutions to seriously complex management challenges.

The emergence of a society-wide focus on skills and technical capabilities is creating the space in the market for individuals to differentiate themselves and is giving rise to a wave of differentiated individual entrepreneurship.

And of course that individual talent can become visible through the utilization of Cyber Economics enabling platforms that bring tremendous efficiency gains to professionals who are looking to extend their service offerings to several companies, instead of selling out to just one employer.

As individual differentiation develops, the dynamics of Cyber Economics support that the financial incentives are of such nature that an increasing number of people will rapidly establish their own personal brand in which the market can trust, and start selling access to their skills on an independent basis, forever leaving behind the role of employee.

The fundamental change from a work force to a skill force is one of the key transitions currently being operated in the marketplace as companies adopt the dynamics of Cyber Economics and a critical element to the comprehension of the full extension of the impact that Cyber Economics will have in society.

Independent, differentiated, highly qualified people see companies they provide services to as Clients and expect to receive equal-foot treatment from the companies they provide services to, openly rejecting the hierarchical elements of employment.

Furthermore, differentiated professionals active in Cyber Economics markets seek challenges that present opportunities for them apply and grow their skills, instead of searching for jobs. Actually, highly differentiated professionals do not even want a job at all, as they perceive a job as be too limiting of their full potential.

And because highly differentiated professionals are independent service providers who do not want a job at all and instead seek personal development, often the teams they integrate with other professionals end up assuming very specific talent centric dynamics that are apt to generate significant value not only for those hiring the services, but also for each of the team members individually; with the advantage that each of the team members gets to incorporate for themselves what was learned for future projects.

That is the reason why the new skill force is rapidly substituting the historical workforce, as independent workers constantly seek personal improvement as a means of remaining competitive and differentiated in the open market where they see themselves as individual start-up companies managing their own Cyber Economics enabled business.

Business leaders who oversee companies adopting the dynamics of Cyber Economics understand these dynamics and implement strategies that prioritize the establishment of one to one relationships with highly skilled individuals acting as true external providers; and assist many of the former company employees to free themselves from the shackles of their former jobs and embrace the incentives, freedom and independency associated with starting their own personal businesses and personal brands.

Personal branding becomes therefore a key element in the professional development of highly skilled individuals active in Cyber Economics.

As highly specialized people realize that they are their own personal brand, they realize that each individual stands for something and has a completely unique skill set that is openly known in the market and can be tremendously valuable to several companies, not just one.

Ultimately, highly skilled professionals realize that, since they are their own brand, they have no need to feed other brands and when this logical step occurs in their minds they take a giant leap towards freedom and independence.

TRUST AND REPUTATION

A company's reputation is a valuable asset – and this is a significant understatement.

Reputation is the key to gaining trust from the general public, from the company's Clients and stakeholders, from government officials and regulatory bodies and is often synonym of the ability to constantly attract and retain profitable relationships.

Being perceived as highly reputed is a fundamental element of any company's ability to thrive in a competitive market. People will commit to companies in which they can trust, and that is one of the fundamental reasons why a positive reputation is a source of great power. Most people will openly admit to love a company's products more if the company's reputation is stellar.

A company's reputation therefore has enormous economic significance. The sheer free-enterprising aptitude of any company, its ability to freely explore new markets and launch new products and its ability to trade and make money is directly impacted by its reputation. Companies with better reputations are inherently more successful as a consequence of having increased access to good will and shared resources and receiving support from others that allows the company to operate inside market support mechanisms at a level that it could not occupy otherwise. As a consequence of all the support received, companies that enjoy elevated levels of reputation are more productive, often exceed expectations and end up contributing to the improvement of society.

Elevated levels of reputation significantly enhance the ability to benefit from future possibilities and assist in creating the conditions for the company to take risks in pioneering new solutions which bring progress and technological advancement.

And of course companies with higher reputation levels are better able to minimize the impact of downturn periods in the economic cycle, while also being more capable of deflecting criticism from management missteps or operational mistakes.

All of this is lovely, but reputation is a fragile asset that requires deep humility to foster and keep and is especially prone to being damaged by arrogance, falsity and hubris. This is the case even for companies that have yet to embrace the digital transformation, but it becomes paramount for companies who are participating in the dynamics of Cyber Economics.

You see, a company's reputation is massively amplified at a global level through the dynamics of

Cyber Economics. It is hard to describe just how very powerful and important the company's reputation is in the digital interconnected world and how much it impacts the company's attractiveness, public image and ability to inspire trust.

Reputation, which is inherently a very fragile asset, is so very fundamentally important in the digital world that business leaders need to really start looking at reputational issues as absolutely central to the company's strategy.

The good news is that Cyber Economics and the adoption of digital transformation have the ability to transform a well-reputed company into a global star, bringing it to unimagined levels of success. The amplification effect that computer networks and social media have on the awareness of the public in general about any given company can elevate a respected, trusted company with a stellar reputation to an ultimate level of hypnotic charisma and fame with respect to its products, its team and even its shareholders.

Companies with elevated levels of global reputation and charisma stick out from the crowd at a global level; they have a certain cachet that others simply do not have and are allowed by market participants to assume relevant positions in society.

Ultimately, the unique level of trust that companies with elevated reputations enjoy means that these companies can have the rare luxury to plan for the long term and introduce disruptive technologies that not only act in the company's interest but also allow the company to reshape the way people live their lives.

A company's reputation is a very fragile asset, which is nurtured only by truth, ethics and integrity, and little else matters.

When a company's reputation is not correctly understood as a truthful reflection of the reality of the company's capabilities and the way it operates, then it could happen that a stellar reputation is harder to develop and maintain.

As the dynamics of Cyber Economics become pervasive in society, reputational risk, which emanates from any potentially weaker links in the way the company operates, is therefore a key focus for business leaders embracing the digital transformation. To put a complex reality simply – risks to a company's reputation materialize when mismatches occur between expectations and truth.

Not surprisingly, in order to manage reputation risk, the company needs to be very real, approach issues with tremendous integrity and ethics and communicate truthfully in all circumstances.

Some of the worst mistakes that businesses fall prey to materialize when companies do not have an ethical approach to their businesses and a coherent, effective and truthful communication strategy in place to reflect that approach, or when they simply decide to not communicate at all.

The dynamics of Cyber Economics are such, that if a company does not own its communication strategy, the communication will nevertheless occur, and be led by others who may not know the truth about the company and may not always keep the best interest of the company as their foremost concern; in which case the company will lose the ability to influence what is being communicated and assure that the truth is well told.

In a digitally connected world, society in general will keep permanent vigilance of all companies and will be especially focused in assessing how these respond to crisis circumstances. Everybody knows that difficult circumstances, mistakes, issues, challenges, unpredictable accidents can all occur. However, in and of themselves, unfortunate circumstances do not directly impact a company's reputation. What will significantly impact a company's reputation is the way that the company reacts in difficult situations. More in particular, the company's reputation will be impacted by it's actions during challenging times not only in what regards the solutions found, but more importantly what the process and outcome really says about the way that the company approached the matter. It is that "modus operandi" that the company adopts to deal with unforeseen circumstances that will show what the company is really all about and hence impact the company's reputation.

That is why business leaders managing reputational risk in digitally interconnected markets need to have full commitment with ethics, integrity and truth. The commitment to truth at management level is inspirational and empowering and therefore is immediately absorbed by the entire organization. When proceeding from a position of commitment to truth, then the toughest of all management challenges can be tackled in a way that is perceived by the outside world either as in line with expectations or even exceeding expectations. This occurs not because the expectations were artificially managed, but because the stellar behavior adopted positively surprises the world and has the effect of feeding a positive loop of reputation reinforcement.

Business leaders who are conscious of the value and fragility of reputation pro-actively use digital resources and AI to identify pressure points or issues across the organization that must be dealt with before they escalate to a level where they can harm the company. In this light, many potential reputational risks end up being addressed internally at early stages, being subject to remedies in order to prevent them form impacting the company's reputation.

Because digital resources store enormous amounts of data and are able to analyze it and integrate the data with other machines, business leaders can look to digital resources to monitor performance, prepare for incidents and even simulate what would happen and how the company would react in crisis scenarios.

Digital resources also have the ability to tremendously speed up and improve the quality of a company's reaction in crisis situations, especially if the company already has a plan in place to deal with challenging circumstances. Fast reaction times, execution of previously thought out contingency plans, controlled approach to the problem mitigation and solving processes and the immediate establishment of audit trails of all actions implemented, when combined with truthful communication, are supportive to the company's reputation.

The nature of Cyber Economics is therefore such that it has the potential to amplify a company's reputation, for good or bad, but it also empowers business leaders to detect early warning signs and triggers of challenging circumstances at a time when these can be dealt with; and of course it also can be put to use to significantly enhance the company's capacity to deal with challenging circumstances.

Business leaders who thoughtfully integrate digital resources with their company's reputation management strategy are therefore rewarded with a profound increase in their power to prevent, ultimately deal with, and successfully overcome circumstances potentially damaging to the company's reputation.

RISKS AND REMEDIES

Business leaders take decisions every day in analogue contexts, fraught with uncertainty and constantly seeking to identify and understand risks in order to implement viable mitigation and management strategies to these risks, and ultimately decide weather to take these risks at all.

Like all technologies, digital resources are artificial constructs that can be used in helpful ways to promote society's advance, but they can also be misappropriated, misunderstood and managed in ways that can prove to be less helpful or even harmful.

And of course, a healthy dose of skepticism is always welcome; so let's look at the five most fundamental risks that Cyber Economics presents to business leaders.

The first risk of Cyber Economics is alienation. Digital resources are hollow, synthetic and operate based on the limited digital framework. Digital machines do not recognize or respect natural order or natural law; rather they are unable to understand the essence of nature, our connection to it and the uniqueness of natural cycles, instead assuming that the future will be exactly the same as the past, which of course is nonsense. That is the foremost risk of Cyber Economics – the risk that business leaders rely so heavily on digital resources that they forego their unique human relationship with nature, natural cycles and the universe as a whole.

The remedy for the risk of alienation through Cyber Economics is creativity. The ability to create or invent something relies deeply in our relationship with nature, natural cycles and the universe. Finding a different way, trailing a new path, disregarding traditional ideas, concepts, relationships and patterns requires deep connection with reality and the ability to use its subtle manifestations to create different outcomes. Business leaders who keep contact with reality, with their communities, are better equipped to steer organizations into offering creative solutions that can be supported by digital resources, but are not limited to them.

The second risk of Cyber Economics is artificiality. The deceptive simplicity of artificiality can be very attractive, but the outcomes it produces are inherently unfulfilling. This risk materializes when business leaders start taking decisions that lead organizations in to producing fake outcomes, with dire consequences. When business leaders allow themselves to become so immersed in the artificial digital realm, they effectively become helpless.

The remedy for the risk of artificiality through Cyber Economics is complexity. While refusing to be limited by the simplistic outcomes offered by digital resources, business leaders who contemplate the complexities of human nature are better equipped to develop business solutions that incorporate digital resources as part of a wider, holistic perspective of value creation.

The third risk of Cyber Economics is removal from the present time. Digital resources can capture, store combine and analyse data, and communicate such data, over large computer networks. However, unlike humans, digital resources are unable to compute the notion that future outcomes are not inevitably similar to the outcomes registered in past occurrences in apparently similar circumstances. Digital resources can compute, but lack the human mental skill of awareness; the cleverness of the human mind that allows it to be in the present moment and take all the present context into consideration. Regardless of how advanced they might be, because of the nature of the digital realm, machines are inherently unable to take into consideration all the complex subtleties of the present moment and its interaction potential, which could only be captured in an analogue world. Therefore, digital resources are unable to assess all the variables of the present instant as they influence future outcome.

The remedy for the risk of removal from present time through Cyber Economics is dexterity. Business leaders who keep their organizations gracefully moving, foster a sense of readiness and flexibility in their organizations, which is key for their ability to adapt to present circumstances.

The fourth risk of Cyber Economics is social isolation. The formation of cyber social networks, which digital resources facilitate, have the ability gently draw people away from personal human interaction and fundamental human support mechanisms, such as spirituality, real community interaction, real friendship, physical presence, interest in society as a whole, interest in family and family interaction, creative cultural expression, etc. All the digital resources surrounding people inside their own homes not only have the power to destroy privacy boundaries; under the guise of "convenience" and over supply of entertainment, it also can make people become isolated from their families inside their own homes. In such cases, people do not talk as much as they did and hence over time, incrementally, their intimacy is reduced, all in the name of an arguable quest for numbed down "convenience" or "comfort". Real community involvement, true friendship crafter from personal interaction, family and shared family life and real love can only be experienced through highly rich first hand personal interaction, not through electronic means. By spending so much time interacting with digital resources, people could forfeit the opportunity to spend quality time with family, friends, and community, thereby losing access to human support mechanisms. Those who allow themselves to become overtly immersed in the artificial reality of social networks, spending so much of their time in the limited digital world, risk becoming dumbed down and become less able to properly function in the real world.

The remedy to the risk of isolation through Cyber Economics is empathy. Empathy is the human ability to fully understand at a deep emotional level what other humans are experiencing. Because of their digital nature, machines are unable to identify and understand personal circumstances, feelings, emotions and motivations. Machines are unable to attribute feelings to objects or relationships. Business leaders who seek to keep a human touch and a level of empathy inside their organizations, are better able to avoid becoming isolated from the Client communities they are serving and are better equipped through empathy to react positively to even the subtlest of changes in customer psychology.

The fifth risk of Cyber Economics is the unprecedented accumulation of individual data. Permanent digital interaction could lead people to disclose and unwittingly hand over all of their thoughts, all their actions, all their private data, including emotional expressions, choices, ambitions and desires to whoever is managing the digital resource collecting the data. The Internet of things, social networks, telecommunications, location services, self-driving vehicles, computerized medical records, facial recognition systems in public places, and all other forms of digital data collection are gathering vast amounts of personal information. Public and private data centres storing personal information will of course do what the digital framework is good at doing – harvest as much information as becomes available from any point of the network, store it in one single place, organize it and subject that information to analysis by AI. The risk is therefore that, through the interaction of AI with vast amounts of personal information, digital resources could be used to interfere with people´s decisions in a meaningful yet undesired way, by impacting people´s ability to think independently, exercise free will, analyse independently, comprehend complex sets of data and execute planned actions, which over time can damage the individual's brain, incrementally curtail choices and erode creative potential.

The remedy to the risk excessive data mining through Cyber Economics is moderation. Business leaders will at some stage be compelled to weigh the economic and social costs of having accumulated too much data from their Clients. Gathering, storing, maintaining and analysing massive amounts of data is tremendously costly from a purely economic standpoint. Moreover, regulatory demands regarding the management of personal data will only become increasingly stringent. And then of course elevated amounts of data will be harder to treat, and the output of the treatment of such data will likely have significant noise. Finally, as society evolves, the ethical implications of excessive collection and storage of private data will be perceived by society as a sign of weakness of business ventures and gradually have the effect of repealing customers, instead of serving them well.

Considering all of the above, we realize that Cyber

Economics like every other technology can be tremendously helpful; as long as business leaders are aware of the risk it implies and take decisions that ultimately protect their businesses and societies in general. Successful business strategies in Cyber Economics will always consider the risks and their antidotes, as they harness the power of digital resources for the good.

At the end of the day, humanity does not need digital resources to prosper - we got here without them in the first place. But of course we can and will use these resources wisely to improve our businesses and empower our societies.

INDUSTRY SPOTLIGHT
AGRICULTURE

Agriculture was traditionally seen as a serene, tranquil activity where stability and peacefulness reigned. Throughout centuries, agriculture was arguably one of the least innovative industries in the world, the epitome of low tech and slow development. Even the mechanization of agriculture that emerged with the industrial revolution did not really fundamentally revolutionize the farming business; rather it mostly made it more efficient and productive.

The inherent dynamics of Cyber economics is

impacting the agriculture industry in such a fundamental, structural way that our perception about farming and our relationship with food will be significantly transformed in a near future.

Many perceived agriculture as a high-risk activity mainly because agricultural output and quality would fluctuate significantly depending on many factors that were thought to be out of the control of farm managers. But that perception is now changing as the increasingly productive farm is becoming less idyllic and more like a modern automated factory.

As the dynamics of Cyber Economics become a reality in agriculture, farming is rapidly becoming a highly predictable, low risk industrial activity, through the effect of the deployment of digital resources.

The new generation of young leaders gradually assuming management responsibilities in agriculture businesses was born with a computer in their hands, is permanently online and is enthusiastic about digital transformation.

Digital savvy business leaders in agriculture are creating a new, cutting edge paradigm of data driven farming, reinventing the entire value chain of agricultural products.

Consequently, in the near future, agriculture will rely so heavily on digital resources that it will evolve into becoming more of a differentiated service providing activity and less of a commodity producing activity.

Let's start by looking at the farm itself.

The next generation of farmers is creating the digital farm. What this really means is that digital resources are being deployed in farms, which effectively allow for decision-making based on real time data.

Digital sensors are being installed throughout farms to permanently collect real time data about a multitude of parameters, such as weather conditions, humidity, sunlight exposure in different areas of the farm, water availability, plant greenness and many other key elements impacting the decision making process.

As digital resources are gradually being deployed and integrated, farm managers own an exact level of detail and control regarding everything that is happening to the farm's production, which they can then put to use to maximize yields.

Being able to know and understand what is happening across the farm increases efficiency to previously unseen levels. Effectively controlling the farm and being able to monitor and register it's status performance on a permanent basis, not only promotes much higher yields and reduces risks, but more importantly, it also harmonizes production and significantly elevates the quality standards of the final product. The entire life history of a vegetable for example, from seed to harvest, can now be registered in digital format, which makes the entire production traceable, and subject to review.

Further to increasing crop yields and overall quality, the standardization and control of the production process allows for the introduction of high value added niche products, which would be too risky or too expensive to produce in uncontrolled environments.

And because so much data is now available for treatment, artificial intelligence is gradually entering the farm and begins taking independent decisions based on the accumulated data. Just like what happened with factories, robots will be executing an increasing number of daily tasks in the digital farm. As an example, artificial intelligence is now able to control water, temperature, and humidity across several sections of the farm, deciding how to use water or when to deploy automatic machines such as seed planters or harvesting robots, depending on the exact conditions on the ground.

Through the use of artificial intelligence, producers are now able to control quality across the entire production process, while taking significant steps to protect the environment, for example by eliminating waste of water thereby preserving water resources, or by applying only the necessary amount of chemicals to protect crops, thereby protecting ecosystems and promoting health across the food chain.

The entire food chain is currently being subject to digitization, and will soon become completely monitored and controlled by digital resources, with relevant impact for society as a whole.

Through the adoption of the dynamics of Cyber Economics, food safety becomes a paramount focus for the industry and a non-negotiable requirement for the consumer.

The level of trust that a farmer is able to offer the

final consumer becomes an unprecedented differentiator as farmers are gradually becoming able to trace the entire food cycle, from the moment it is planted to the moment it is consumed.

As the food chain becomes completely monitored by digital resources and subject to effective controls, blockchain technology will be used for marketing purposes.

Through the implementation of blockchain technology across the entire food chain, consumers can be effectively reassured of all the steps that their food went through until it came to their plate.

Consumers will therefore be served with guaranteed trust, guaranteed provenance, and product differentiation.

From a marketing standpoint, the application of blockchain technology will also create the opportunity for the story behind the product to be told in the context of marketing efforts, adding valuable context and meaning to the consumer experience.

Packaging is another fundamental part of this process.

In the past, agricultural products would ship out of a farm in unsophisticated containers, were transported in often less than ideal circumstances, and would reach the consumer with unstable, unpredictable quality levels.

But Cyber Economics is also coming to the packaging industry. Today's informed consumers demand sustainable packages, which adopt innovative ways to display and preserve food and allow the consumer to know the entire lifecycle of the exact product at hand as a key factor in the making of purchasing decisions. One basic requirement for food packaging today is that it contains a QR code or other digital interface, which can be scanned with a smart phone, offering instant information about the product, how it was made, the choices that the producer made, and the differentiating elements of the specific product when compared with competitors.

Modern consumers are spending less and less time preparing their meals, and are stocking items in their pantry or refrigerator for much smaller periods of time than in previous generations. The impact of packaging in the way that consumers make choices is tremendous, not only does packaging create the kind of trust relationship that will make consumers repeat purchases, but also smaller, easier to open, more ecological packages are potentially more likely to draw the preference of the modern shopper.

And this is just the beginning for food packaging. With the gradual adoption of the Internet of Things, many families and institutions are purchasing smart refrigerators. These refrigerating machines are actually computers with the capacity to know what is available in the refrigerator box through digital recognition technology. Food packaging is now gradually including digital transmitters, which establish the communication between the package and the refrigerator. And because the refrigerator is connected to the Internet, and quite likely has some form of artificial intelligence as part of its software, the computer running the refrigerating machine will be able to know all about the product by connecting to the producer's website.

Then everything is coming full circle for the agricultural business.

For the consumer, a new world of convenience and trust is opening up. Digitally connected refrigerators are becoming capable of informing of when it is the best time to consume a certain product before it loses freshness, they can also suggest recipes that make the best out of the ingredients at hand in coordination with pre-programmed nutritional requirements and preferences of the consumer, and of course the refrigerator may receive permission to independently order more of a certain food item when it is consumed.

Through the implementation of Cyber Economics in the agricultural business, the consumer will enjoy better quality food items delivered directly to the comfort of their home; benefit from full trust in the entire food chain; become empowered to make better diet choices; eat more nutritious food in adequate portions; avoid accumulating leftovers; and procure food items directly from the producer completely cutting off the several intermediaries operating in the food industry with the consequence that the food items will cost much less than they would if purchased in a supermarket.

Therefore the agriculture business gradually transforms into a highly specialized, fully consumer oriented, digitally run industrial activity, in which marketing assumes paramount relevance and the promotion of fundamental values such as food safety, traceability, freshness, and quality assume their role front and centre in business development, as farmers seek to establish their own differentiation which allows them to create and maintain a long-term trust based relationship with each of their individual Clients.

And since the consumer is ordering directly from the farm, is keenly aware of what is being purchased and cares about who the producer is and is watchful of the reputation that the producer enjoys; then food is no longer a commodity anymore.

Now that the consumer becomes involved and really begins to care about how food is produced, value added services can be incorporated in the farm's offering, such as tailor made agricultural products, catering to the Client's specific needs, such as slow food, niche products, fully organic production, specific species, etc.

Business leaders active in the agricultural business

who lead the adoption of the full circle of Cyber Economics in their farms by creating Client centric agricultural businesses will reap enormous rewards.

Not only will farms produce more with less costs, much higher quality and much lower risk, but the farming business will establish a long-term relationship with the consumer.

This one to one relationship will then flourish over time as the consumer's habits and preferences become known to the farming business.

And of course because the consumer becomes involved and excited about food, many innovation opportunities will be discovered through the permanent mining of the available data regarding consumer preferences, allowing for the previously unimagined deep customization of agricultural products.

Cyber economics is therefore a tremendously powerful dynamic that will impact agriculture by imposing structural changes to the farming business that will completely reshape the way we relate with food.

INDUSTRY SPOTLIGHT
ARTIFICIAL INTELLIGENCE

One of the basic laws of our universe is that everything is connected with everything else. There is no way anything can be outside the universe and what appears to be chaos merely means that we are coming from a limited perspective.

What this means for those who occupy leading positions in the business world is that, in order to broaden our perspective and act in alignment with the truth, we are called to first exercise our ability to discover exactly what the truth is, so we can be aligned with it.

And it turns out that, just like a diamond in the rough, often the truth is hidden and must be unearthed and treated, or in the case of a diamond lapidated, to be brought up to its magnificent splendour where we can put it to good use.

When we finally gain awareness of the truth, when we unearth it, we can align our actions with it and become tremendously powerful. That is the moment of clarity, when we truly become empowered to deliberately impact the world around us effectively through the expression of our creativity.

In that sense, we can say that our creativity is unleashed by our ability to correctly assess and properly weight the numerous aspects and subtleties of the truth, and then envision a new, better way forward.

All of us have experienced in our own lives that we attract success effortlessly when we are finally able to recognize the truth of what we are and any situation we are immersed in, making ourselves available to serve something greater through our intervention, instead of focusing our energy at whatever our petty little egos just want without connection with reality.

That is where our role as business leaders will be enormously empowered by artificial intelligence (AI) – The promise of AI seems to be to assist in aligning us with the truth in a wide number of circumstances.

One of the hottest topics for today's business leaders is the discussion about the impact that AI, automation and robotics will have in the near future.

Today, everybody and their mother are talking about AI, either approaching it as the final Holy Grail, or as the facilitator of the arrival of doomsday when machines would rule over a destroyed humanity. None of these visions is aligned with the truth. What will end up happening is that AI will empower humanity to take a giant leap forward.

AI has been around for a while, but now it is becoming a mainstream topic as a consequence of the expansion of the Internet of things, the gradual adoption of oral discourse as the increasingly preferred means of interaction with machines, and the growing concerns of the public with data security and privacy, emerging from several recent incidents.

But before we get over excited about AI, let's get real about what AI really is and is not, what it can and cannot do and especially how its power can be unleashed in a controlled, helpful way so that we can begin to understand how AI will be of service to us as we lead the way forward in business.

Allow us to be a bit provocative here – as the next decades come by, business leaders who work with AI will gradually become much more effective than those who do not, because they will be more able to align themselves with the truth and act creatively based on their better perception of reality. And so it makes no sense at all to look the other way and think that AI is some geek thing that will not impact your life – it will, so deal with it.

When we are talking about AI, we refer to the ability that a digital resource may have to independently assess of "learn" how to perform a certain task, without requiring human intervention specifically instructing it exactly how to proceed.

AI enabled digital resources are machines which use large amounts of data, analyse it and extrapolate. Programmers tell the machine which data to review and analyse, and then instruct the machine to solve a problem based on the analysis that the machine made.

The larger the set of data, the more likely it is that the machine is able to identify patterns in the data and effectively "learn" to offer solutions to recurring problems.

For example, a machine could be instructed to analyse a relatively wide set of photos and then identify certain common traits in the people or places appearing in those photos, which in turn would make it more capable of improving recognition of the same place or person in different circumstances.

Today's computational capacity is so developed, that this can be done with unbelievably large amounts of data.

Furthermore, as the outcome of one assessment made by AI is produced, it can instantly be shared with other interconnected machines. As an example, a surveillance camera at the entrance of an office building could be connected to a computer, which in turn has access to the photo database containing photos of the faces of all the people who are allowed to work there. Once someone comes up to the entrance, and the camera captures her or his face, the computer can compare the image from the camera with all the images on the database and decide to grant access to the facility. However, if the computer is also connected to the schedule of all of the company's employees, it could identify that this person works at the office, but is supposed to be on holiday, in which case admittance to the office will be denied, or if the machine is so instructed, it can allow access to the office building, and notify the Human Resources department that this specific person came to work on that day, so that perhaps the person is awarded a compensation day off.

So what did the machine do?

The machine used access to several databases in real time to effectively make a decision based on past observations and other inputs. In reality, AI can be much more effective than this and make much more complex associations, but by grasping this mechanism you now have a workable notion of what AI is and how it works.

Effective AI would be impossible without data and without large processing capacity. AI works best with big data behind it, makes better assumptions when it has constant input that allows the machine to establish a likelihood of a certain outcome; and requires very advanced computers with significant processing capability, often interconnected in a network of machines.

Not surprisingly, we will see AI become more prevalent first in areas of life where machines are already collecting large amounts of data, because that is the fertile ground that AI needs to flourish and produce better outcomes.

But make no mistake – as time goes by machine learning will impact all areas of the economy and become one of the fundamental elements of Cyber Economics.

What AI will ultimately do is simplify, automate and reveal the truth.

Simplification means that AI works marvellously in all sorts of repetitive assignments where a significant number of iterations can be taken into consideration. This would be the case of many administrative and operational functions in today's businesses, where many of the tasks can become fully automated and processed by digital resources running AI technology. This can and will fundamentally change the way companies run key repetitive processes and will impact the way business is done on a daily basis. This will also release many people in the workforce from repetitive functions and give those who desire to expand their horizons an opportunity to move to more personally rewarding and creative roles.

Automation does not mean that everything becomes automatic with AI. Rather, it means that over time machines, which will work hand in hand with humans but not independently from them, will handle much of the really uninteresting tasks. The reality of automation is that machines will work best when the creative or specialized or contextual part of the work being made is completed under the supervision and in collaboration with humans. That is what we mean when we say that AI will become our best friend.

And finally, AI will assist in revealing the truth in those cases where it will be able to recognize patterns in big amounts of data and offer business leaders the ability to see the truth that was previously buried under the mountain of apparently useless information.

As the adoption of AI becomes pervasive, companies will unleash innovation capabilities which were previously lost in inefficiencies, building on all the empowering information made available to management teams through the deployment of AI.

And unlike what many have tried to suggest, AI will not lead humanity to a life of permanent pleasure and abolish any need for us humans to do any work. Quite on the contrary, what AI will do is empower humans to do more qualified, more specialized, more technical, less repetitive, more creative and more productive work. We will be able to produce much more and gravitate to unimaginable levels of achievement.

But of course AI is by all means not a panacea, it is just technology, which means that while it has significant merits and will become ubiquitous; nevertheless it still has significant limitations. When people refer to AI they often forget to mention its true nature and limits, and what it can and cannot do.

One of the fundamental differences between us humans and AI enabled machines is that we are autonomous learners and we do not require large sets of data to be able to come up with an educated guess about how to solve a problem. Machines are unable to solve problems about which they do not have historical data.

AI enabled machines will assume that the future is always a repetition of the past and will take decisions extrapolating from the data made available to it by previous iterations. However, these machines are unable to explain the rationale behind the decision. Basically what the machine is doing is to express the most statistically probable adequate reply to a given problem, based on previous observations.

This statistic basis of AI of course works fine in a controlled environment, but is prone to all sorts of mistakes when the AI is let out in the wild where the variables are unlimitedly abundant, which means that AI should be deployed with care in more sensitive areas of life and even then should be monitored by humans. It also means that because machines will not be able to explain the rationale of their decisions, issues will inevitably emerge about liability for unintended mistakes and their consequences emerging from the fact that machines are unable to deal with contextual information simply because of their digital nature.

History often rhymes, but rarely repeats itself. The fact that, in the past, in a certain context, life occurred in a certain way, by itself does not present any guarantee that the future will always operate in the exact same way.

Furthermore, because of the limited nature of the

digital framework – which is composed of 1's, 0's and disregards all that is in between – the data that the machines have at their disposal is inherently less complex and infinitely poorer than reality itself. Regardless of how great the machines become in taking decisions extrapolating on past data, they will inevitably risk failure to provide the appropriate answer simply because the machine is unaware of the entire complexity and fullness of reality.

Machines to not have conscience. Only humans do.

It is comforting to realise that that by adopting AI humanity will not risk losing control of life on earth to machines. What AI will do is remove us from the weight of dealing with unfulfilling parts of everyday work, and work in tandem with us humans in dealing with complex circumstances.

And therefore business leaders have nothing to fear from AI, because machines are inherently unable to lead.

In turn, humans will become much better leaders when supported by AI, because AI will be able to analyse enormous sets of data that humans would never be able to have the time or patience to go through, and that will make human intervention much more powerful, and decisions much more spot on.

In the end, that is how AI should be used – in coordination with the human mind and conscience, aiming to empower humans, not challenge them.

INDUSTRY SPOTLIGHT
EDUCATION

The widespread adoption of the dynamics of Cyber Economics throughout society inherently establishes personal improvement as a development target.

Through the massive adoption of digital resources and the commoditization of information, the entire education process will shift from information sharing to the promotion of technical expertise, creativity, collaboration and problem solving.

Both the ability to develop rare skills and the ability to

completely master common skills at an elite level will become unique differentiators for individuals.

In a digitally mature society, formal education provided by academic institutions such as universities will represent only a part of the personal improvement market, as a plethora of new skills enhancement providers, which can range from all sorts of coaching to skills based courses in any activity ranging from cooking to rally car driving assume their roles in the skills developing process.

For the economy as whole, what will matter most is that individuals will spend more of their time developing new skills or bringing those skills they already achieved to the next level.

In mature Cyber Economics markets, mentors assume new relevance, as people seek access to the masters and their guidance in any skill in order to achieve their personal development milestones.

Many opportunities will therefore present themselves

to business leaders who wish to be a part of society's efforts towards expanding the skills development market.

In turn, what this means to business leaders managing education institutions is a complete refocus of existing learning programs and the repositioning of academia from traditional educational providers to lifetime partners for those individuals focusing on enhancing their skills to elite level.

By doing so, not only will formal education continue to rely heavily on digital resources as teaching tools, but also many of the educational experiences on offer will be made available, at least partially, through electronic means.

Educational institutions will not longer offer educational programs as such, instead they will offer learning experiences that immerse individuals in learning groups, promote diverse approaches to problem solving and provide ample opportunity to apply skills in effective, practical contexts.

Teaching will evolve from the previous experience of one teacher lecturing a classroom, to the development of direct learning relationships between lecturers and small groups of individuals in a relationship of proximity and mutual exchange.

Consequently, the dynamics of Cyber Economics will transform university programs in less academic focused, tutorial based experiences and more into project focused, team based programs, aiming at developing practical skills.

As a result, education will no longer be seen as something people are required to be devoted to in exclusivity for so many subsequent years at the early stages of life.

Children will continue to spend their infant lives and adolescence in learning contexts and rooted in formal education and academia. But as they grow up, while going through formal education, young people will also be engaging in significant learning experiences and acquire sets of skills that will be considered effective differentiators to their personal brands.

As we are all benefitting from increasing life expectancy, we will therefore continue our learning path throughout our entire lives.

INDUSTRY SPOTLIGHT
FASHION

Fashion remains somewhat of a paradoxical industry.

While the fashion industry as a whole attracts some of the most creative minds on the planet and the fashion world is in constant change as trends and collections come and go at ever-increasing speeds; the not so obvious reality in the fashion business is that the industry infrastructure is dominated by very large players that benefit from significant barriers to entry, contributing the establishment of what has effectively become a very stable and profitable industry structure for incumbents and an extremely risky activity for tentative challengers.

But the dynamics of Cyber Economics will hit the core structure of the fashion industry in ways still unsuspected to many.

Let's start by looking at the role of the challengers who will circumvent barriers to entry and get into the action in different ways.

Operating independently through the use of digital resources, independent designers become empowered by the use entrepreneurship support platforms to start disseminating their unique perspectives.

As consumers and consumer groups start offering real, effective feedback to independent designers about what they would like to experience in their individual fashion choices, independent designers can reach out to crowd funding platforms to assist them in establishing their brands.

Orders for "capsule" collections created in articulation with buyers can be accepted through online websites long before production starts, clearly stating that production will only occur once a certain threshold of sales is guaranteed.

Just like in other areas of society where assets are not utilized to full capacity, many factory owners will be willing to offer manufacture capability to small collections for much lower costs through the use of digital resources.

And since the entire capsule collection is sold before manufacturing, it can be directly sent out from the manufacturer to the consumer, thereby eliminating warehousing requirements.

Marketing small designer collections through social media can bridge the gap between designers and the consumer by enabling trust based connections without the need to attempt to access the large online distribution platforms for post manufactured goods or large physical retail locations.

Digital resources will therefore empower business leaders seeking to enter in the fashion industry to create ecosystems of designer support that will gradually open larger portions of the market to independent designers.

Designer support ecosystems will be very welcome by the experiencing seeking consumer who will for the first time be able to influence the final product and request individual specifications before it is produced that are not available in the post production market, with the exception of haute couture ateliers charging prohibitive prices.

As independent designers develop their brands, they will further the use of Virtual Reality (VR), Augmented Reality (AR) and Mixed Reality (MR) to assist in marketing efforts as the customer will be able to try, and with MR manipulate, many different styles before taking decisions, which creates the conditions for a continued offer of unique products tailored to the individual.

Because more and more fashion will be ordered before it is produced, body scanning applications will assure that the exact proportions of a person's body are accurately measured and that fashion always fits perfectly, effectively enhancing the customer experience through the democratization of mass tailoring.

For the industry as a whole, the widespread adoption of technology by the consumer will also bring numerous changes in the relationship that people will establish with their fashion.

Wearable technology is becoming mainstream, not only with watches but extending from eyeglasses to headphones and even garments.

Then, as most of the search engine queries will become oral or image based, consumers will be able to instantly purchase any fashion items they see anywhere just by describing it to their smartphones or by pointing their cameras at the object.

Furthermore, as several online outlets will be offering the product and many other similar competitive products, price competition will be fierce.

Big brands will also have increasing difficulty in controlling the emerging fashion influencers, such as bloggers, simply because as their audiences grow larger they will be rewarded for independence and free analysis and not by pushing merchandise as they did in the early days.

Independent, trusted influencers with large follower bases will become a serious force to deal with in the industry, but they will effectively seek to distance themselves from the big players exactly as a means to build trust with their base.

Fashion also produces enormous inefficiency. Just think about all the clothing items you have in your wardrobe or storage space that is completely not utilized for long periods of time.

As with many other areas of society, Cyber Economics enabling platforms will offer the public in general the opportunity to market used products that still have inherent value, either for resale or for limited use, with the effect of deviating many consumers away from new purchases in all segments of the market.

Pay per use is also coming to fashion, especially hitting the luxury segment for many high cost clothing items, with similar success as in other industries.

Again, the consumer has little interest in owning a highly expensive collection of fashion items. What the consumer is looking for is the experience of enjoying the use of these items and then not having to deal with them as legacy after the experience has come to an end.

As an example, a consumer who does not usually get invited to black tie parties may occasionally receive an invitation to one. Instead of purchasing the fashion outright, through the use of peer-to-peer platforms and using body measurement software to check suitability, the consumer will be perfectly well fitted in a few minutes through the rental of the appropriate outfit for the party without having to disburse large amounts of money to purchase it.

The significant psychological change that is coming to society as a consequence of the adoption of digital resources will therefore challenge the role of the existing large brands in many ways.

The first challenge is that the combined application of all these technologies is inherently deflationary.

As people rent fashion, less high-end product will be sold; as people buy capsule collections from independent designers, large players gradually lose their market share; as people follow independent influencers such as fashion bloggers, directing the purchase impetus through influence control becomes much more difficult; as people search for an item in all online outlets simultaneously, including new, used discounted, alternatives and rental options, selling items becomes harder; and as independent designers use factory downtime at zero risk, big players with pre-established manufacturing and warehousing capabilities may suddenly have to deal with overcapacity and inventory.

Big players in the industry will then be tempted to cut back on costs, for example using machine bots to manage customer services and reduce marketing efforts, with the effect of having to restructure at a certain stage.

This entirely new paradigm in the relationship between the consumer and the brand means that the retail store is going to change dramatically.

For certain fashion items in which the origin and quality of the materials used are paramount in justifying the price level, fashion brands will begin using blockchain technology to certify authenticity.

And finally, from being the place where the consumer goes to buy whatever standardized products were available, the retail store will transform into a socializing place where people hang out, experience the values of the brand, interact with products and services that the brand is offering either in person or through the use of in-store technology, and may or may not purchase any items at all.

INDUSTRY SPOTLIGHT
FINTECH AND BANKING

The dynamics of Cyber Economics are completely changing the financial industry.

Banks in particular will emerge from the digital transformation as more efficient, technologically advanced, consumer-focused entities; but will retain a fundamental role as trust hubs in a much more decentralized financial system.

We will start by addressing the consequences of the adoption of digital resources in the banking sector;

then we will look at the vibrant opportunities presenting themselves everyday in the Fintech space; and we will conclude this part of our business strategy book by looking at the consequences of the widespread adoption of blockchain technology.

What very few people will tell you about banking is that, under the appearance of extreme sophistication and cutting edge product innovation, the truth of the banking industry has always been one of slow change in core banking activities.

The banking industry has historically operated on the basis of the following three pillars: (i) regulatory protection, (ii) ability to retain talent, and (iii) ability to retain Clients through the control of extended distribution channels.

When combined and all wrapped up with excellent marketing, these three traditionally sustaining pillars of the banking industry have been the key enablers of trust, which fostered the establishment of long-term relationships between banks and their Clients, and have guaranteed that business continued as usual in the banking industry.

Even the early days of the Internet have not really impacted the core of the banking activity as much as people were led to think, as bank managers have mostly seen web and mobile technologies as distribution channels.

Web and mobile technologies, being client facing technologies, became IT investment priorities to the banking industry and have absorbed significant part of IT spending in banks for most of this century, while structural investment in many of the core banking systems lagged. Many banks still rely to a certain extent on legacy structures and software for core banking functions, and consequently middle-office departments, being inherently dependent on legacy core banking systems, also lag in efficiency as a consequence of years of cost control in non-client facing parts of the banking business.

But all this is about to change as the dynamics of Cyber Economics take banking by storm.

Let's look at what is happening to each of these three support pillars of the banking industry.

As a consequence of the impact of digital transformation throughout society, regulatory protection that was traditionally the first support pillar of banking has morphed into regulatory pressure and activism, seeking to crack open the existing business model of banking enterprises, stripping the banking activity to its core, and pushing banks over the edge into the new digital world of open banking.

On one hand, as a means of preparing banks to adopt digital transformation, the regulatory framework applicable to banking became more stringent through the adoption of new standards applicable to bank capital adequacy, stress testing and market liquidity risk; with the ultimate goal of reducing the ability of banking managers to put institutions at risk through elevated risk appetites.

On the other hand, by leading the banking system into an open banking architecture, regulators are creating the conditions for the emergence of a new business context for the banking industry in which data is shared amongst several non-related financial industry players through application programming interfaces (APIs), making service capabilities that were traditionally reserved to banking become available to many other players in the market place.

The first consequence of open banking is the consumer centricity that emerges from the added control that banking Clients will have over personal data, which of course will bring forward better consumer experiences, financial services provider choices and lower costs.

Bank account holders will now become empowered with the authority to instruct their banks to share their personal financial data in real time with other financial services providers, thereby scrapping the banking world's monopolist rule on financial data across the financial services spectrum.

As a consequence of open banking, many business leaders seeking to enter into the financial services sectors without having to operate through banks are now shaking the market with a vast amount of technologically based financial services companies, which we will aggregately refer to as Fintech.

The second traditional sustaining pillar of banking, talent retention, is under significant challenge through the application of the dynamics of Cyber Economics.

As banks become closely regulated, and compensation limits are imposed on management teams as ways to curb risk appetite, many banking executives will seize the opportunity to become independent and find more appropriate valuation to their personal skills in other parts of the financial industry, by effectively investing in their personal brands and providing their services independently to the fast moving ecosystem of technological companies seeking to become active in Fintech.

Furthermore, as a consequence of open banking, most banks will find it extremely difficult to hire and retain balanced and functional IT teams that can assure all the developments required to many of the banking legacy IT systems; and will consequently face significant challenges in the restructuring of their non-client facing operations teams, in which people will require a completely new set of skills to be able to drive the new operational framework required by open banking.

The third traditional sustaining pillar of banking, the ability to retain retail Clients and small to medium enterprises (SME's) through the control of extended distribution channels, is deeply compromised by the inherent dynamics of Cyber Economics.

Traditionally, Clients had a relationship with their relationship manager at branch level, who was the bank's main financial product placement interface with the Client, focused mainly on placing products offered by the bank.

For private banking Clients and SME's, more sophisticated account managers with wider toolboxes placed more sophisticated products; and to a varying extent, some of the products placed by private and SME bankers were offered by entities not affiliated with the bank, in which case the bank functioned and was remunerated as a financial intermediary.

But with open banking, the consumer will enjoy the ability to rely on technological financial services providers – Fintech companies – which are not focused on placing products at all, rather are interacting with the Client in real time situations where financial services are seen as enablers of consumer experiences and not so much as products, reacting to consumer input.

Consequently many of the professionals that were previously retained in employment relationships with banks, and have developed personal finance skills, will seize the opportunity to leave the work force and join the skill force, thereby becoming independent asset managers and independent certified financial advisors serving Clients directly instead of serving financial institutions as client facing employees.

Consumers who have adopted lifestyles reflecting the dynamics of Cyber Economics are less interested in owning a certain financial product and much more focused on using financial assets as means to access whatever experience they are focused on at any given moment.

That is where the market space is opening up for Fintech companies.

By exploring the opportunity to access client data through open banking, Fintech companies are able to offer a wide range of consumer centric services, which can include instant payments, crowd-funding of projects, peer-to-peer lending, credit scoring, credit facilitation services, asset management and direct trading.

The emerging financial system will inevitably become decentralized from an operational perspective, deeply interconnected, much more efficient and completely consumer centric.

As the financial industry focuses more on the consumer and less on bank offered products, new service propositions will emerge as a consequence of individual or group demands.

As the adoption of the dynamics of Cyber Economics unfolds, banks will therefore become less relevant as financial industry players, will be seen by many as utilities, and will lose their current ability to control many of the consumer´s choices as the financial market evolves into a more efficient, decentralized structure.

Blockchain technology will also have a striking impact on financial services as a consequence of its ability to create trust and scarcity in the digital world.

Blockchain technology establishes a ledger, which can be defined as a book of final entry where transactions are recorded for accounting purposes.

Information contained in the ledger is then organized in blocks.

Once each block is completed, it is backed up in a chain of blocks organized in chronological order – the blockchain – and subsequently a new block is created.

All the information inserted in the blockchain is subject to encryption as a means to preserve the integrity of the data, which effectively creates an indelible, unchangeable entry.

The blockchain is publicly distributed and accessed by any member of the community in real time. Each digital resource (node) connected to the blockchain receives direct real time access to read the full blockchain right from inception; which means that every single transaction vested in the blockchain can be traceable, audited and validated by the community and that all information is public.

In laymen's terms, this means that all the transactions you participate in, which are registered in a block chain, are public for everyone to see.

Business leaders active in the financial industry are currently investigating the many potential uses of blockchain technology as a means to guarantee certainty and trust in digital transactions.

The main strategic impact of the blockchain for the financial industry is the introduction of tamper-free technology, which can be used for many purposes whenever trust and authenticity of the records generated is key.

As an example, payments can be directly executed in real time between participants of a blockchain system without the need to collect an authorization from a financial intermediary, such as a bank.

The transaction is executed directly without the need for third party intervention and is subject to record in the blockchain where it remains permanently documented and is publically distributed as the blockchain contains all the information regarding all the transactions for its entire history since inception.

The strategic impact of the adoption of blockchain technology in middle office operations is significant and will lead to strategic changes in the way accounting and payments are processed in the financial industry; clearing the way for deep operational automation with significant cost reductions in accounting systems and operational head-count while greatly eliminating errors and repetitive double check requirements.

And because blockchain technology can be used to demonstrate all the assets each participant held at any given time, and to identify all the transactions that each participant has participated in; the widespread adoption of blockchain technology by entities operating in the financial industry will be able to deploy efficient and effective anti-money laundering actions, with tremendously positive consequences in financial crime deterrence, detection and prevention.

Seed capital is currently flowing in large amounts into solving some of the implementation issues of blockchain technology, which include addressing issues related with execution speed and storage of the entire blockchain as it grows ever increasingly larger at elevated speeds.

The ultimate frontier in the adoption of blockchain technology will be crossed when governments and central banks finally decide to create a global sovereign backed crypto-currency, most likely as the outcome of global coordination under the leadership of the International Monetary Fund (IMF) as an evolution of the present Special Drawing Rights (SDR), based on the assumption that under the new currency arrangement the ability of central banking authorities to intervene is assured and the complete security of the entire currency can be guaranteed with sovereign level cyber security tools.

When that occurs, the role of banks as custodians of currency will evolve to a new role as guardians of the trust in the distributed blockchain.

As a consequence of the adoption of the dynamics of Cyber Economics, the banking sector will then continue executing the fundamental role as trust enablers to the entire financial system by assuming decentralized responsibility in the maintenance and management of the distributed blockchain, admitting and certifying the participants in the blockchain and offering transaction validation services to the community while continuing to compete with Fintech players in the rendering of financial services across decentralized networks.

INDUSTRY SPOTLIGHT
HEALTHCARE AND WELLNESS

In a context of ever increasing costs and demographic pressure, business leaders overseeing companies active in healthcare industries have been deploying digital resources for a long time as a means to promote efficiency gains, but the overall results have fallen short of ambitions and expectations because the system continues to operate in an exceedingly centralized, inefficient way.

Not only do the already elevated costs with healthcare continue to rise, but also the increasing adoption of digital resources has even, in some cases, negatively impacted the consumer experience by adding procedures and complexity in the name of quality.

The core reason behind this failure to achieve the full potential of digital transformation in healthcare can be found in the way that medical records are collected, treated, accessed and deployed.

But the status quo can be challenged by the adoptions of the dynamics of Cyber Economics to promote a trusted way to manage medical records.

Following a similar script as the one currently being adopted by financial services regulators, and building up on newly adopted stringent personal data protection rules as a base, health regulators could launch an open health framework in many ways similar to the above described, and already deployed, open banking framework, although with additional data protection and digital trust safeguards.

In a nutshell, open health would mean legally

recognizing the right that each citizen could have to instruct any holder of her or his medical records to grant real time access to those records to other entities legally operating in the healthcare field, for the benefit of the individual.

But regardless of how relevant financial data inherently is, medical records are a much more sensitive information, and must be treated as such; which would imply that additional control measures should be assured in the process of granting access to medical records to any entity.

The solution to assure trust, security, encryption and decentralized access to medical records data would likely to be found in the adoption of blockchain technology to the safekeeping of medical records through the creation of a sovereign managed and hosted blockchain based medical records registry.

In a blockchain based open health framework, the medical records information contained in the blockchain would be completely encrypted by default and each individual could be granted the right to exactly decide which records should be made available to which providers, in which conditions, and which records should be kept private.

Consequently the specific data identified by each person would then be deciphered and made available to the specifically identified health services provider acting in the best interest of the individual.

Under an open health framework, government agencies and emergency care medical professionals would legally retain the full right to access the entire individual blockchain based health records whenever their intervention would be necessary.

Once blockchain-based medical records become available to health tech companies as a consequence of the personal decision to disclose them, an explosion of health tech services would ensue which would combine medical records, data from wearable devices and artificial intelligence to effectively monitor individual health.

And of course the data collected by the wearable devices would also be loaded to the blockchain and become available for future use when needed by any authorized party.

For the consumer, Healthtech would represent a completely new, much more rewarding way of experiencing individual healthcare, wellness and personal health monitoring.

As a means of furthering security of the data, the blockchain itself would be permanently monitored by the sovereign authority managing the entire system through the deployment of AI, which would also use machine learning to complement the ability of the blockchain management system to generate on demand individual health reports based on the entire blockchain based medical history of the individual, making these reports available in clearly defined contexts to the individual, to government officials and to medical professional in possession of authorization or acting in face of medical emergency.

The immediate consequence of the sovereign adoption of an open health framework would then be the significant reduction of the pressure over existing services, the enabling of distance consultations, distance diagnosis, distance prescriptions and permanent monitoring and stabilization of long-term conditions.

Many visits to hospitals would be avoided, especially for monitoring purposes, effectively delivering previously deemed impossible system wide efficiency gains and cost cuts while promoting individual health responses of unique quality.

The longer-term consequence would be the empowerment of the individual to actively participate in the management and monitoring of personal health, by experiencing the advantages of an individual, digitally assisted health management plan.

Permanent monitoring of personal health through interconnected wearables, Healthtech and AI in an open health framework, will also have the consequence of making individuals active participants in their health improvement and responsible for their health outcomes.

In certain non-compliance cases, failure form individuals to collaborate with prescribed therapies could lead to decisions to suspend public subsidies or insurance policies to individual treatments as a consequence of non-compliance from the individual with prescribed health and life supportive therapies.

Ultimately, society as a whole will become engaged in the promotion of better health habits and more sustainable lifestyle, and the consequence will be significant increases in productivity, overall happiness and longevity.

INDUSTRY SPOTLIGHT
INSURANCE

The insurance industry will be deeply transformed through the adoption of the dynamics of Cyber Economics.

From being used to running a slow motion, mostly predictable business, in only a few years business leaders overseeing companies active in the insurance business suddenly found themselves in extremely dynamic, unpredictable contexts.

The banking industry has historically operated on the

basis of the following three pillars: (i) regulatory protection, (ii) slow motion market dynamics and incremental change, (iii) well-known standardized risks.

As a consequence of the combination of these supportive factors, the insurance industry became quite significant.

Slow speed combined with stable profits and predictable risks enabled an accommodative stance in many insurance industry leaders, who have delayed reform in key areas such as dynamic risk management and middle office operations.

Just like in banking, web and mobile technologies did not crucially impact the core of the insurance business as most of the IT investments conducted over the last decade by large insurers have been applied to client facing activities, while middle office reform and product innovation have lagged.

All of this is now changing at breath-taking speed.

Just like we did with banking in an earlier chapter of this book, let's look at what is happening to each of the three support pillars of the insurance industry

Following the same script as in banking, insurance regulators are increasing capital requirements to insurance risk carriers, requiring more stringent risk taking as a means to curb risk appetite of management teams.

The new approaches to risk management and increased capital requirements directly impact profitability and, just like with banking, push companies over the edge into the speedy adoption of the dynamics of Cyber Economics as a means to preserve shareholder return and profitability.

Insurance regulators are also in the process of gradually separating insurance carriers from certain client facing distribution activities as a means to push insurance carriers to focus on digital distribution methods and direct insurance.

By effectively losing control of direct distribution networks and tied insurance intermediary sales forces, insurance carriers lose the ability to influence pricing and drive sales volumes, with the effect that insurers now face deep differentiation challenges until they finally adopt a deep digital transformation strategy.

The second traditional sustaining pillar of insurance, slow motion market dynamics and incremental change, is now completely gone.

Let's look at the different areas of insurance activity to identify the fast motion market dynamics currently introducing disruptive change to the insurance industry.

Auto insurance is going through a profound change emanating from the combined effect of autonomous vehicles and telematics. Over the next few years, the use of autonomous vehicles will become widespread in society, with several deep consequences.

Today, most of the car accidents are attributed to human error and disrespect for driving rules. As autonomous vehicles become pervasive, after an initial period of uncertainty during which the technology is perfected, over time a significant reduction of car accidents will occur.

Car ownership will also change. As cars become autonomous, the consumer will not be interested in owning a vehicle to keep it idle all day. Instead, car manufacturers and specialized companies will operate fleets of autonomous vehicles; with the effect that car insurance becomes a commercial product line and not a personal product line, with the immediate effect of reducing premiums.

Furthermore, as autonomous vehicles will be used to higher levels of capacity, and will therefore circulate much more often that privately owned cars, existing actuary assessments of the inherent risks in car insurance will have to be remade from scratch.

Finally, even in the case of drivers who retain their own cars and choose to drive them, telematics will be used to exert downward pressure on insurance premiums.

This disruptive evolution in car insurance will then be followed by the appearance of new risks that will require immediate coverage such as cyber security of autonomous vehicles, product liability for manufacturers of autonomous vehicles and infrastructure insurance related with autonomous vehicles, such as high speed electricity chargers.

Property insurance will also be disrupted by the widespread adoption of digital resources in real estate.

Residential property insurance will be impacted by the evolution of the use of property emanating from the utilization of Cyber Economics enabling platforms that generate higher capacity utilization of the property, but also bring new risks, such as the liability of the owner of the property towards any guests for damages caused by the property; or damages incurred in the property through the presence of guests in the context of a commercial arrangement.

Commercial real estate insurance will also be impacted by the emergence of the virtual office, as many people will rent offices by the hour for a plethora of different commercial activities, each with it´s own risk profile.

In the health insurance business, disruptive changes will emerge from Healthtech, on which we have elaborated above in connection with health monitoring wearables.

From an insurance perspective, these disruptive technological developments in health monitoring will significantly impact the pricing models for health insurance.

As many people will leave the work force and join the skills force, as discussed above in detail, increase demand will become apparent for income protection insurance for individuals; providing protection against credit default and lifestyle loss, effectively establishing a personal safety net in the case of loss of income will become a significant business opportunity for nimble insurers.

In traditional life insurance, increased longevity and Healthtech will disrupt current actuarial tables and require different risk assessment metrics in order to quantify risks and correctly define premiums in the context of extended contractual maturities.

The current beginning of a new bear super cycle in bonds in the context of higher interest rates going forward implies that company owned investment portfolios could go through intense scrutiny and rebalancing as a means to manage duration risk. On the other hand, the upwards momentum in the interest rate cycle will re-open the annuities and guaranteed capital products markets, which had been closed since the financial crisis as a consequence of the zero and negative interest rate policies adopted by central banks.

In and of itself, the return of interest remuneration would of course be wonderful news for insurance carriers, but the competition for shorter term capital allocation coming from both the Fintech and banking sectors in a context where insurers have lost control of distribution networks, will require creative thinking regarding how to offer old school solutions to a present-focused, highly dynamic and more informed consumer. Furthermore, an always connected, highly informed consumer will challenge the idea of bearing the risk of the balance sheet of the insurance carrier for long periods of time, especially when Fintech operators and banks will be offering direct ways to invest in underlying assets without having to add a layer of balance sheet risk on top of the investment risk inherent with any investment.

Retail oriented unit-linked products will face headwinds as a consequence of the expected scrapping of tax breaks to all kinds of long-term investments, as sovereigns seek to put capital to work in the short term to assist in reforming their economies and enhance taxable opportunities.

However, two major markets will remain extremely dynamic for private placement life insurance (i) executive compensation as a consequence of the most talented people leaving the workforce and joining the skills force and (ii) succession planning for high net worth individuals (HNWI) and ultra-high net worth individuals (UHNWI) as a consequence of the quick disruption of the traditional concept of family and the emergence of the global entrepreneur, with assets and significant personal relationships spread out over multiple jurisdictions.

The third traditional sustaining pillar of insurance, well known standardized risks, is also compromised by the dynamics of Cyber Economics.

As a consequence of the widespread adoption of the dynamics of Cyber Economics, insurers will not be able to wait sufficient time for standardization of risks to occur before they are compelled to underwrite.

This disruptive development will put an emphasis on the monitoring of risks, especially when large risks are considered, through the use of digital resources, and will be yet another force towards imposing automation and AI monitoring to the management of insurance books.

The good news for insurance carriers is that digital resources will be able to significantly elevate the insurance carrier's ability to manage and monitor risks, through the adoption of blockchain technology in articulation with AI.

Insurance activity is based on contracts and full compliance with these is a crucial element of risk management.

For many years, one of the most damaging risks to insurance carriers has been abusive litigation by Clients seeking to find breaches in contract terms alleging inadequate compliance with those terms as a means to abusively imposing liabilities to the insurance industry.

One of the supportive elements of abusive litigation against insurers emerged from circumstances in which insurance carriers did not fully and exhaustively document all of it interactions with Clients, thereby losing ability to prove having fully complied to contractual duties and having rendered adequate servicing when prompted for.

However, all this can change through the deployment of digital resources to the automation of insurance carriers operations, as one very interesting application of blockchain technology is the possibility to create smart contracts.

Smart contracts are one of the most interesting applications emerging from blockchain technology and the insurance industry will most likely adopt them rather quickly.

For context and capabilities of blockchain technology, we refer to the comments included above in this book regarding the blockchain, how it operates, its benefits and the consequences of being a decentralized, distributed resource.

In the case of insurance, blockchain technology can be distributed to middle-office servers inside the company, to the Client, to any brokers involved in the transaction, and to the regulators, all in real time.

A smart contract is a string of computer code that can be inserted in the blockchain defining the exact terms of any agreement.

Once the smart contract is created, all interactions between parties related with the agreement – either that be proof of payment of a premium or the full recording of a phone call or internet interaction between the insurer and the Client – can be added to the blockchain for later reference, thereby establishing an effective, permanent, exhaustive audit trail of the entire relationship established between parties for the duration of the contract which can be used as proof of compliance.

And of course, like any contract, smart contracts can include terms that determine certain actions under certain circumstances.

When any of these circumstances is met, the contractual term is immediately executed through the deployment of digital resources, without any human intervention being required.

As an example, in a life insurance smart contract, when the death certificate of the assured life is added into the blockchain, and all conditions required to the processing of the payment to beneficiaries are met (such as their identification and their banking data), the payment of the death benefit can be triggered instantly and automatically.

Since the blockchain, and the smart contract, is stored in any computer in the network, all parties and the regulators know at any given moment that contract execution is correct.

Furthermore, insurance carriers can then use AI technology to permanently monitor the evolution of all the smart contracts in the blockchain in order to assure effective compliance and regular behaviour patterns and signal out deviant patterns, bringing up exceptional or otherwise deviating cases to the attention of analysts, with the purpose of fighting insurance fraud, abusive claims and assuring stellar levels of service.

The consequence of the inevitable adoption of blockchain and smart contract technology by the insurance industry, under monitoring through the deployment of AI, will be deep automation of operational functions and the significant reduction of abusive litigation.

Ultimately, insurance companies will become deeply automated companies and the insurance industry in general will become leaner and much more profitable.

INDUSTRY SPOTLIGHT

MARKETING AND THE CONSUMER

The dynamics of Cyber Economics and the deepening pervasiveness of digital technologies in all areas of life are changing the requirements of the consumer at breath-taking speed.

In markets where the adoption of Cyber Economics has matured, individual services based on trust and reputation become key, as the consumer is increasingly looking for an experience, not simply a product or a service.

It will not even be enough for the consumer to be spoiled with choice – only the ability to enjoy an individual experience will cut it.

The shopping mall culture, as we know it, is dead.

The idea of a zombified consumer roaming endless corridors of mostly insufficiently differentiated stores pushing product at elevated prices, drooling at what the masters of consumerism have prepared for the masses, only to eventually being led to choose from a limited set of standardized products waiting in the storage room to be picked up and taken home as a trophy, has finally come to an end.

The reason for this sea change is of course the adoption of the dynamics of Cyber Economics and the arrival of hyper connectivity, Virtual Reality (VR), Augmented Reality (AR) and Mix Reality (MR) to the consumer.

VR is a technology capable of generating immersive experiences creating for the user the illusion of being inside a certain digital context.

AR is a technology capable of bringing digital imagery into your surroundings.

And MR is a technology that allows you to manipulate virtual, digital objects while mixing them with your real surroundings.

Flagship smartphone models today come equipped with VR and AR engines, and as soon as processing and battery capacity allow for it they will also be able to process MR applications.

What this means is that the entire marketing of consumer products and services will shift to an experience based approach.

Through the interaction with VR, AR and MR technology enabled digital platforms made available by leading companies, consumers will be able to effectively craft their own individual products and services and share these with others.

Or even better, consumer groups will be able to build the services and products that ideally fit their needs by interacting with brands through VR, AR and MR.

For the first time in history, the consumers will build products and services for their individual needs.

Marketers will no longer assist brands in downloading their products and services by adjusting communication and positioning to certain segments – instead, marketers will assist brands in positioning themselves as the most efficient and trustworthy suppliers of the individual experiences that the consumer is looking for.

As the dynamics of Cyber Economics develop, the once inconceivable alliance of brands with consumers becomes a reality, as companies and their clients team up to create unique experiences, and brands become supporters of individual lifestyle requirements.

The emergence of experience consumption over the now defunct off the rack consumerism, as a consequence of the massive adoption of the dynamics of Cyber Economics, will forever change the mind of the consumer.

The consumer will have zero interest in owning most assets, if any, simply because these will be available to experience at very reasonable prices whenever needed through the usage of Cyber Economics enabling platforms, which maximize efficiency across the entire economy.

As the experience economy deepens, society as a whole becomes heavily focused on combining maximum efficiency with the most flexible experience.

In a context of individual experience crafting and pervasive access to information, self-improvement will become another driver for the consumer.

Many people will reach out to technology to use their time more effectively, which of course includes improving oneself in order to enhance the differentiation and competitiveness of the personal brand.

As an example, people will quickly adopt self driving cars simply because they will free up enormous amounts of time, during which people will not have to care about driving, and will be free to read, access online education or participate in virtual group meetings aimed at enhancing their skills.

In a context of hyper connectivity, big data and AI, brands will profoundly shift the way they interact with the consumer, leaving behind traditional advertising and moving towards the delivery of personalized, instant offers as soon as signals of potential interest become apparent.

Ultimately, the consumer will seek and achieve a previously unimaginable level of joy in consumption, emanating from the uniquely personally pleasing nature of the products and services made possible through the adoption of the dynamics of Cyber Economics.

INDUSTRY SPOTLIGHT
REAL ESTATE

Cyber Economics is deeply impacting real estate, as the new keyword in this traditionally rigid market is now flexibility.

Starting with the supply side, looking at real estate development, the dynamics of Cyber Economics are deeply shaping investor choices as many investment opportunities are currently being identified, and quantitatively assessed, through the use of digital analytics tools.

Through the use of digital resources, real estate developers are able to identify which are the fastest growing areas for each kind of product in the markets they are taking into consideration, and are also able to credibly quantify the demand for a certain kind of product in a certain location.

Better-informed investment decisions typically produce lower risk outcomes and reduce time to market.

Once the investment decision is implemented, real estate developers are deploying extensive use of digital resources in the product planning stages going as far as to include the detailed visualization of the product being conceived through the use of virtual reality technology so that experts can simulate the relationship that users will establish with the final product once it is built, and a wide array of details and flexible options can be considered well before construction starts.

Still in the product conception stages, developers

planning real estate products for markets adopting the dynamics of Cyber Economics are currently designing buildings for super-connected, highly flexible use.

Building planners are also heavily focused on bringing automation and AI to building management, with the purpose of enhancing the quality of the final product and significantly reducing the environmental impact of the project, regardless of what the various uses that the building will be subject to throughout its entire useful life.

As construction work starts, digital resources are omnipresent throughout the construction process as a means to promote security, control execution, comply with regulations, promote quality and facilitate project management within pre-defined parameters.

Finally, as the real estate product is coming to the market, commercial activities are deployed through the use of digital marketing techniques, again putting an emphasis on flexibility and quality of the marketing process; assuring that the right people are correctly informed about the investment opportunity represented by the product, and that several flexible options in terms of space occupation and contractual relationships are made available to encompass the widest possible array of different utilization needs.

Still on the supply side, real estate investors who have not developed the product but already own it are benefitting significantly from the adoption of the dynamics of Cyber Economics by reconverting their properties to enable flexible utilization, automated management when applicable and enhanced connectivity.

As previously outlined above in this book in further detail, in recent years real estate owners have gained access to significant efficiency gains in the management of their real estate investment portfolio through the widespread adoption of Cyber Economics enabling platforms,

As we consider the real estate demand side, let us

start by addressing the profound changes that Cyber Economics is bringing to non-residential real estate markets.

Companies that adopt digital transformation strategies and embrace the dynamics of Cyber Economics require a completely new, more efficient, technologically advanced and flexible relationship with the real estate they occupy for their operations.

Manufacturing companies who have adopted the dynamics of Cyber Economics have reconverted most of their production lines to deep automation through widespread adoption of robotics and AI.

The adoption of deep automation and AI deployment in the manufacturing process significantly impact the real estate requirements of these companies not only in terms of the amount of space required but also in the quality, flexibility and overall connectivity and accessibility of the building, that also need to operate at the highest possible quality and security standards.

Companies with significant office requirements space are completely rethinking the office as a consequence of embracing Cyber Economics by considering office space as mostly a team collaboration venue and productivity-enhancing hub.

Companies that have embraced digital transformation have completely reshaped their offices in such a way that these become flexible work support venues while in the process granting workers many different ways to deliver their contributions.

The adoption of the dynamics of Cyber Economics enhances the mobility of all the people in the organization in such a way that offices become social spaces where people work and totally differ from the sweat shops of the past.

Companies active in the retail sector remain conscious of location of their stores but are applying the dynamics of Cyber Economics to reshape customer experience inside their retail outlets.

Today's customer can interact with the company through a wide array of digital resources any time, anywhere. In such context, retail spaces become flagships, where Clients can become immersed in company culture, values, products and ways of doing business that far exceed the mere function of being a place where the company's products are available for sale. In the context of Cyber Economics, the retail store has been deeply transformed into an experience venue, with deep consequences in the way that the real estate product where the store is installed is conceived and executed.

And finally, as we consider real estate demand, let us address the profound changes that Cyber Economics is bringing to residential real estate markets.

As we become ever more busy as a consequence of being permanently connected to the world, our homes also embrace Cyber Economics and we start surrounding ourselves with many network enabled digital resources which are commonly referred to as the Internet of things. These resources can go from refrigerators to televisions to window shutters to computerized temperature controllers and everything else that turns a residential space into a smart home and provides provides comfort and convenience to users on a daily basis.

In order for the Internet of things to function properly and integrate seamlessly, today's residential real estate is expected to offer the highest possible connectivity and flexibility.

Cyber Economics dynamics also changed the way we work and go about our day. Today most people do at least part of their work from home and this requires that home office spaces are available for the several inhabitants of the space to feel confortable and productive in.

And because more and more people are increasingly working from home at least some of the time, living areas inside the home are called upon to offer a wider range of leisure and socializing areas.

As the home is used for longer periods of time, residential energy consumption has been increasing significantly and many families are requiring that sustainable energy sources are installed in their homes.

The apparatus of digital resources that can electrically malfunction combined with art and many other valuable items justify a new heightened concern with physical security of modern homes and with protections against intrusion.

As a means to deal with all these demands, real estate developers undertaking new construction or rehabilitation are working together with Clients right from the project stage in order to enhance the flexibility of the product and incorporate all the specific requirements of each buyer, effectively producing tailor made homes.

Cyber Economics will gradually influence the way that contracts involving real estate are drafted through the adoption of blockchain technology, which provides secure, auditable technology that will automate the valuable work of both notaries and public registries.

Finally, the dynamics of Cyber Economics are also operating in the wide array of flexible options in which residential real estate is offered in the market, which can vary from outright ownership, to time sharing, to fractional ownership, to guaranteed return buy to let, to many different kinds of mortgages and leases which can span from very short periods to very long timeframes.

When all the abovementioned changes in real estate as a consequence of the adoption of the dynamics Cyber Economics are taken into consideration, the outcome is a much more flexible, friendly, efficient, convenient, experience focused and tailor-made reality.

INDUSTRY SPOTLIGHT TRANSPORTATOIN AND SMART CITIES

The gradual adoption of the dynamics of Cyber economics creates unique opportunities to transform our cities into safe, sustainable spaces with increased environmental quality, fostering new levels of quality of live and socialization.

As all sorts of objects receive digital connectivity capacity, the Internet of Things (IoT) is coming to town and will create the conditions for our cities to function in smart, interconnected ways.

In order to promote the proper functioning of high-speed, high-latency citywide connectivity, smart cities actively engage with telecommunications providers in finding solutions that foster hyper-connectivity inside the city limits.

One of the first and foremost areas of immediate impact of IoT in large cities is applied to scarce water resources management. Water storage centres are monitored closely for availability and quality and sensors deployed around the city will be able to instantly address leaks in the water distribution system, and smart irrigation systems will keep parks green and inviting, while effectively reducing waste.

Security will be another fundamental area of impact of the arrival of the IoT to the urban space.

Large cities where millions of people interact and potentially enter into conflict everyday pose a variety of significant security risk to individuals, property and to the function of infrastructure.

Through the use of interconnected security sensors with a swarm of both fixed, drone-based, vehicle based and even body based surveillance security cameras, all interconnected with face recognition enabled AI systems, central operational city security centres will be able to effectively monitor the daily life of the city and effectively deploy security forces, firemen and medical resources in the shortest period of time to anyplace inside the city where these resources are most needed.

The same technology can be applied to the pre-emptive dispersion and management of crowds in order to assure the security of people and assets in the vicinity of crowds right from the moment when these are in the process of forming.

Interconnected cities will also be better prepared to react in case of natural disaster or any other form of calamity through its ability to rationally deploy relief efforts to the most critical areas.

Through the deployment of AI technology analysing the mobility flows of people inside its boundaries, smart cities planners will be able to identify which areas should be reserved to each specific kind of use (residential, sports and leisure, office, commercial, warehousing, parks), seizing opportunities to mix people and organizations as a way to effectively and harmoniously spread people across the city as they go about their different activities, thereby avoiding centralization of functions in specific areas with unhelpful consequences in terms of mobility.

Great cities to live in will empower inhabitants get actively involved in city management through the use of e-government and mobile government platforms, effectively partnering with inhabitants in shared design and deployment of city policies.

And of course great cities will embrace the trend towards pervasive use of digital resources in transportation to create intelligent ways to assist seamless mobility inside the city.

As a starting point, government officials in charge of mobility of smart cities are seeking to make them more walkable and more bikable through the adoption of several initiatives, which include granting free digital access to unlocking pre-charged electrical bikes.

In an ideal city, cars would be parked outside the city limits and people would walk around, bike around, or use public transportation.

But since the goal of eradicating cars from cities is incompatible with the goal of retaining citizens and their business from moving elsewhere for convenience reasons, smart cities are taking a holistic approach to individual transportation and instead are taking steps towards a holistic management of transportation.

Through the adoption of the dynamics of Cyber Economics, the emerging trends in transportation in regards to connectivity, electrification and autonomy are significantly impacting transportation.

In the short-term future, cars will be marketed as a service, to be paid by the minute through the use of car sharing platforms accessible through smart phones.

As autonomous, self driving vehicles gradually make their way into the transportation market over the coming years, many of these vehicles will be made available for digital ride hailing, with the effect that people will no longer have to carry their car into the city, as they can simply hail one as desired, and they will be able to enjoy their time whilst inside the time to work or socialize.

Receiving inspiration from the airplane industry, where pilots are required to file flight plans with the air traffic controllers reporting their mobility intentions; Smart cities will also be able to offer digital access to city mobility controllers in such a way as to allow both individuals and means of transportation to connect with centralized AI enabled mobility management digital resources, informing the city management system of what individual mobility requirements are, and receiving in return real time feedback regarding which means of transportation and which path to follow in order to reach the destination in the shortest period of time or with the lowest possible cost.

Finally, as electrification of automobiles finally becomes a reality, smart cities will create the infrastructure required for vehicles to connect to the electric grid, from which these vehicles can purchase or sell electricity.

As a consequence of the combined adoption of all these technologies emerging from the dynamics of Cyber Economics, smart cities will soon become secure, environmentally friendly, safe quality spaces where people will deeply enjoy living, conducting business, socializing and entertaining.

INDUSTRY SPOTLIGHT
TRAVEL AND HOSPITALITY

As the last chapter of our business strategy book, let's look at one of the industries that lead the adoption of the dynamics of Cyber Economics at global level, and assess how it is benefitting from elevated profitability and increased consumer satisfaction by simply telling you the story of what you could do today, actually right now, should you decide to start your next journey on the exact moment you stop reading this book, and what the possible best outcome of your journey could eventually be.

So when you finish reading, go for it.

The travel and hospitality industry has been one of the business areas where the gradual adoption of the dynamics of Cyber Economics has been quicker and deeper.

Through a relentless focus on operational automation, travelling has gradually become more enjoyable and smooth, allowing the consumer to focus on experiencing the journey and not the inconvenience of travelling.

The effect of widespread adoption of digital resources throughout the entire industry has created a staggering growth in efficiency, profitability and volume for the industry as a whole.

The early adoption of smartphone interaction has been one of the keys of success for the travel and hospitality industry. Most users today book their entire travel experience straight out of their mobile phones.

And so our little story starts.

In a few moments, you could start your journey by using your smart phone to use a car hailing service to take you to the nearby airport.

While on your way to the airport, you could use your smart phone to buy an airline ticket, choose your meal preferences for the flight, select your seat and check in.

Then you could choose which hotel you would like to stay in at your destination and immediately select some services you would wish to order immediately, such as for example asking that fresh flowers, mineral water and a fresh fruit basket to await in your room upon arrival. You could also take the opportunity to complete your hotel check in, so that you would not be required to waste time with details upon arrival and just enjoy the experience.

If you would be flying with the airline you usually fly with, and staying with a hotel chain you usually stay with, the entire process would be even faster and with less clicks and you would likely get some added perks like air miles or upgrades.

If instead you would fancy a more authentic experience, you could book to stay at someone's home and it could even happen that the property is equipped with digital key locks, in which case you would receive instant digital access to unlock the door of the place you would call home for the next few days right on your mobile phone, before you had even reached the airport.

And while you would be at it, also before you reach the airport, you could use your mobile phone to go ahead and book several experiences to enjoy at your destination, such as for example a master sushi cooking class with a Japanese chef, a private visit to a wine cellar with a specialist, concert tickets or much more simply you could book a table for dinner at a highly recommended restaurant. If you would be staying at someone's home, you could even go grocery shopping on your smart phone and make sure that your groceries would be delivered to you a little after you arrive.

And of course you could pre-book a car hailing service to pick you up on arrival and drive you to your final destination.

All of this could possibly have occurred today and you hadn´t even reached the airport yet.

At the airport, if you had previously joined one of the fast track screening systems available in several countries, you would be able to breeze through security controls in only a few minutes and proceed straight to your preferred café, do some last minute shopping, or simply head to a lounge where you would enjoy the opportunity to relax, catch up on your reading or just listen to your favourite music.

During the flight, airline staff would address you by

your preferred name and make you as comfortable as possible.

Assuming you would choose to stay at a hotel, once you had arrived at your destination, you could find that your hotel room could be a hyper connected place where you would be surrounded by the Internet of Things, with which you would interact orally to setup a wide number of parameters, which could range from setting your preferred room temperature to asking a little something from the room service menu or simply to select your choice from the pillow menu.

During your stay at your hotel, the staff would address you by name and be aware of your preferences; and not only would they cater to those perfectly, but also they could eventually surprise you with unexpected suggestions and gifts that miraculously align exactly with your taste.

You are in heaven!

The outcome is a natural, fluid joyful experience.

Throughout your journey, you would likely never feel bothered by administrative steps; the seamless interconnectivity of everything would create a completely fluid experience.

That is how rich and rewarding your travel could be today.

Coming back home, you would use your social networks and specialized hospitality platforms to leave your personal impressions and review. The positive and rich feedback you would provide other travellers with, could effectively improve the reputation of the several entities you would have been purchasing services from and assist other travellers into making better choices.

Welcome to Cyber Economics.

Enjoy your journey.

AFTERWORD

When we stared our business strategy book, we were looking for answers to several questions:

- Could it be that digital technology is a mere optimization and simplification tool utilized by society with the aim of assisting us in doing the same things we did before in an easier, more efficient way?

Having read the book, you now understand that this question makes little sense, if any.

Digital technology, in all its simplicity, is

tremendously empowering. It will bring society to a completely new level of efficiency, but it will also allow us all to do many things we had never even thought possible.

- Could something more relevant than mere optimization emanate from the adoption of digital technology that requires deeper consideration in the way it will impact the way the economy works?

Having read the book, you now understand that the widespread adoption of digital resources throughout society is deeply impacting the way the economic works and creating a new economic context, which we refer to as Cyber Economics.

- Could the digital revolution produce consequences that reach so far and wide into the fabric of society that it completely reshapes human interaction on a global scale?

Having read the book, you now understand that the global impact of the dynamics of Cyber Economics is so far and wide that it will, inevitably, reshape the way we interact with each other on a global scale.

BIBLIOGRAPHY

ARI LIBARIKIAN, K. J., DOUG MCELHANEY, AND ANI MAJUMDER. 2017. Harnessing the Potential of Data in Insurance. McKinsey Quarterly.

BARBER, T. 2018. Why Ai Could Be Your New Best Friend. World Economic Forum.

BARDHI, G. M. E. A. F. 2015. The Sharing Economy Isn't About Sharing at All. Harvard Business Review.

BASEL KAYYALI, S. K., AND MADHU PAWAR.

2016. Why Digital Transformation Should Be a Strategic Priority for Health Insurers. McKinsey Quarterly.

BEAN, R. 2018. How Big Data and Ai Are Driving Business Innovation in 2018. MIT Sloan Management Review.

BLAU, A. 2017. The Behavioral Economics of Why Executives Underinvest in Cybersecurity. Harvard Business Review.

BLAU, A. 2017. Better Cybersecurity Starts with Fixing Your Employees' Bad Habits. Harvard Business Review.

BOCCA, R. 2017. 3 Things Countries Need to Do Today for an Energy-Secure Future. World Economic Forum.

BORLAND, J. 2017. Why We Are Still Convinced Robots Will Take Our Jobs. World Economic Forum.

BOURLA, A. 2018. 5 Key Trends for the Future of Healthcare. World Economic Forum.

BRANDLEY, T. B. A. J. 2013. Ten Steps to Planning an Effective Cyber-Incident Response. Harvard Business Review.

BRYNJOLFSSON, E. 2017. How to Thrive — and Survive — in a World of Ai Disruption. MIT Sloan Management Review.

CHITKARA, S. D. E. A. A. R. 2009. The Practice of Global Product Development. MIT Sloan Management Review.

COLLIS, C. C. A. D. 2011. Should You Have a Global Strategy? MIT Sloan Management Review.

COSTONIS, J. C. A. M. 2017. Driverless Cars Will Change Auto Insurance. Here's How Insurers Can Adapt. Harvard Business Review.

CURRY, S. 2017. Boards Should Take Responsibility for Cybersecurity. Here's How to Do It. Harvard Business Review.

DANIEL, M. 2017. Why Is Cybersecurity So Hard? Harvard Business Review.

DAVIS, C. B. A. J. 2012. Learning How to Grow Globally. MIT Sloan Management Review.

DEBRUSK, C. 2017. Five Robotic Process Automation Risks to Avoid. MIT Sloan Management Review.

DESJARDINS, J. 2018. How the Internet of Things Has Evolved over the Last 50 Years. World Economic Forum.

DIBROV, Y. 2017. The Internet of Things Is Going to Change Everything About Cybersecurity. Harvard Business Review.

DUGAS, M. S. A. M. 2017. More Training Won't

Reduce Your Cyber Risk. Harvard Business Review.

EOIN WHELAN, D. M., ROB GLEASURE, AND JAN VOM BROCKE. 2018. How Emotion-Sensing Technology Can Reshape the Workplace. MIT Sloan Management Review.

ERIK BRYNJOLFSSON, D. R., AND CHAD SYVERSON. 2018. Unpacking the Ai-Productivity Paradox. MIT Sloan Management Review.

FURLOW, D. D. A. C. 2017. The Best Cybersecurity Investment You Can Make Is Better Training. Harvard Business Review.

GAGNON, A. D. S. A. C. 2018. Company Organization in the Age of Urgency. McKinsey Quarterly.

GAGNON, G. 2013. Why Businesses Should Share Intelligence About Cyber Attacks. Harvard Business Review.

GANGU, P. 2018. We Need to Approach Ai Risks Like We Do Natural Disasters. Harvard Business Review.

GEORGIOS ZERVAS, D. P., JOHN W. BYERS. 2016. The Rise of the Sharing Economy: Estimating the Impact of Airbnb on the Hotel Industry. Boston University.

GERALD C. KANE, D. P., ANH NGUYEN PHILLIPS, DAVID KIRON AND NATASCHA BUCKLEY. 2017. Achieving Digital Maturity. MIT Sloan Management Review.

GRAY, A. 2018. These Charts Will Change How You See the Rise of Artifficial Intelligence. World Economic Forum.

GREG BELL, C. J., TONY BUFFOMANTE, AND KEN DUNBAR. 2017. Ai Adds a New Layer to Cyber Risk. Harvard Business Review.

HAUSMANN, M. B. U. A. L. 2018. Airfreight Forwarders Move Forward into a Digital Future. McKinsey Quarterly.

HAZAN, J. B. A. E. 2017. Five Management Strategies for Getting the Most from Ai. MIT Sloan Management Review.

HERBOLZHEIMER, C. 2017. Limit Cyberattacks with a System-Wide Safe Mode. Harvard Business Review.

HUCKMAN, R. S. 2018. What Could Amazon's Approach to Health Care Look Like? Harvard Business Review.

HUNT, T. A. A. V. 2018. Accelerating the Diffusion of Technology-Enabled Business Practices. McKinsey Quarterly.

JACQUES BUGHIN, T. C., BRYCE HALL, AND NICHOLAS VAN ZEEBROECK. 2017. Improving

Your Digital Intelligence. MIT Sloan Management Review.

JACQUES BUGHIN, T. C., MARTIN HIRT, AND PAUL WILLMOTT. 2018. Why Digital Strategies Fail. McKinsey Quarterly.

JESUTHASAN, R. 2018. 4 Ways the Rise of the Machines Can Work for Humans World Economic Forum.

JOSÉ ESTEVES, E. R., AND GUILLERMO DE HARO. 2017. To Improve Cyber security Think Like a Hacker. MIT Sloan Management Review.

KAK, S. 2017. Is Artificial Intelligence Set to Become Conscious? World Economic Forum.

KANE, G. C. 2018. Why Companies Don't Respond to Digital Disruption. MIT Sloan Management Review.

KERR, W. R. 2016. Harnessing the Best of

Globalization. MIT Sloan Management Review.

KIRON, D. 2017. What Managers Need to Know About Artificial Intelligence. MIT Sloan Management Review.

KIURT MATZLER, V. V. A. W. K. 2014. Adapting to the Sharing Economy. MIT Sloan Management Review.

KUEMMERLE, W. 2005. The Entrepreneur's Path to Global Expansion.

LESLIE CHACKO, E. S., AND CLAUS HERBOLZHEIMER. 2016. Can You Put a Dollar Amount on Your Company's Cyber Risk? Harvard Business Review.

LIBERT, M. B. A. B. 2017. Could Ai Be the Cure for Workplace Gender Inequality? MIT Sloan Management Review.

MAHLON APGAR, I. 2009. What Every Leader Should Know About Real Estate.Pdf. Harvard Business Review.

MANEY, H. T. A. K. 2018. The End of Scale. MIT Sloan Management Review.

MARTIN REEVES, L. F., KEVIN WHITAKER, AND FABIEN HASSAN. 2018. The Truth About Corporate Transformation. MIT Sloan Management Review.

MCDERMOTT, B. 2018. Machines Can't Dream. World Economic Forum.

MCKINTY, C. 2017. The C-Suite and It Need to Get on the Same Page on Cybersecurity. Harvard Business Review.

MICHAEL CHUI, J. M. 2018. What Ai Can and Can't Do (yet) for Your Business. McKinsey Quarterly.

MICHAEL HOROWITX, W. W.-B. 2018. Academia Can Be an Important Vanguard of the Fourth Industrial Revolution. World Economic Forum.

MICKOS, M. 2018. Train Your Employees to Think Like Hackers. Harvard Business Review.

MORGAN BAZILIAN, D. G. V. The Way the World Produces and Consumes Energy Is Changing. How Can We Meet the Needs of the Future? World Economic Forum.

MUPPIDI, S. 2017. Companies Need More Than Two-Factor Authentication to Keep Users Safe. Harvard Business Review.

NICK HARRISON, G. F., AND DUNCAN BREWER. 2018. Why Amazon's Grocery Store May Not Be the Future of Retail. Harvard Business Review.

NICKELSON, D. 2017. Medical Systems Hacks Are

Scary, but Medical Device Hacks Could Be Even Worse. Harvard Business Review.

NJEMANZE, H. 2018. Why Every Company Should Consider Creating a "Cyber No-Fly List". Harvard Business Review.

OHMAE, K. 1989. Managing in a Borderless World. Harvard Business Review.

PAREKH, A. M. A. E.-J. 2015. How the Sharing Economy Can Make Its Case | Mckinsey & Company. McKinsey Quarterly.

PETER REA, A. K., WENDY RITZ, AND MICHELLE D. STEWARD. 2016. Corporate Ethics Can't Be Reduced to Compliance. Harvard Business Review.

POSNER, B. 2017. Revisiting the Logic of Being Global. MIT Sloan Management Review.

PRABUDDHA DE, Y. J. H., AND MOHAMMAD

S. RAHMAN. 2018. Avoid These Five Digital Retailing Mistakes. MIT Sloan Management Review.

RANSBOTHAM, S. 2017. Accelerate Access to Data and Analytics with Ai. MIT Sloan Management Review.

RANSBOTHAM, S. 2017. Ai and the Need for Speed. MIT Sloan Management Review.

RANSBOTHAM, S. 2017. Are New Advances in Ai Worth the Hype? MIT Sloan Management Review.

RANSBOTHAM, S. 2017. Safeguard Your Organization's Iot Initiatives. MIT Sloan Management Review.

RAY A. ROTHROCK, J. K., AND FRISO VAN DER ORD. 2018. The Board's Role in Managing Cybersecurity Risks. MIT Sloan Management Review.

REED, C. 2017. Here's How Ai Can Make You

Better at Winning Arguments. World Economic Forum.

RICH, B. 2018. How Ai Is Changing Contracts. Harvard Business Review.

ROBU, P. K. A. K. 2016. A Best-Practice Model for Bank Compliance. McKinsey Quarterly.

SAM RANSBOTHAM, D. K., PHILIPP GERBERT, AND MARTIN REEVES. 2017. Reshaping Business with Artificial Intelligence. MIT Sloan Management Review.

SHARMA, K. 2018. Can We Keep Our Biases from Creeping into Ai? Harvard Business Review.

SHUBHAM SINGHAL, B. W., KYLE WEBBER, AND SUSAN NOLEN FOUSHEE. 2017. Where to Compete in Today's Healthcare Market. McKinsey Quarterly.

SRINIVASAN, R. 2017. How Machine Learning Can

Help Identify Cyber Vulnerabilities. Harvard Business Review.

STEENIS, H. V. 2018. Five Things I Learned from Davos 2018. World Economic Forum.

STEPHANIE FORREST, S. H., AND BENJAMIN EDWARDS. 2013. The Complex Science of Cyber Defense.

STEPHENSON, C. J. R. A. W. D. 2013. Cyber Security in the Internet of Things. Harvard Business Review.

SULMEYER, M. 2018. What the Rise of Russian Hackers Means for Your Business. Harvard Business Review.

SUMMERS, S. C. A. L. H. 2014. How Uber and the Sharing Economy Can Win over Regulators. Harvard Business Review.

UNRUH, D. K. A. G. 2018. The Convergence of Digitalization and Sustainability. MIT Sloan Management Review.

UNRUH, D. K. A. G. 2018. How Ai Will Define New Industries. MIT Sloan Management Review.

VERBERNE, J. 2018. Can Blockchain Serve Business, People and the Planet? World Economic Forum.

VICTOR, D. G. 2017. The World's Energy Is Getting Cleaner and Cheaper — but Not Quickly Enough. World Economic Forum.

VINTZ, S. 2017. Cfos Don't Worry Enough About Cyber Risk. Harvard Business Review.

VIVEROS, M. 2013. Cyber Security Depends on Education. Harvard Business Review.

VOGELGESANG, S. J. A. U. 2016. Automating the Insurance Industry | Mckinsey & Company.

McKinsey Quarterly.

WEBER, S. 2013. Four Things the Private Sector Must Demand on Cyber Security. Harvard Business Review.

WEINBERG, J. K. A. A. 2018. Three Questions You Should Ask About Your Cyber-Security. Harvard Business Review.

WILLMOTT, S. M. A. P. 2014. Accelerating the Digitization of Business Processes. McKinsey Quarterly.

WINSON, A. 2018. Using Ai to Help the World Thrive. MIT Sloan Management Review.

WOERNER, P. W. A. S. L. 2018. Is Your Company Ready for a Digital Future? MIT Sloan Management Review.

YAMPOLSKIY, R. V. 2017. Ai Is the Future of

Cybersecurity, for Better and for Worse. Harvard Business Review.

ABOUT THE AUTHOR

For more information about the author, please browse the author's personal website www.antoniobelosantos.com

www.ingramcontent.com/pod-product-compliance
Ingram Content Group UK Ltd.
Pitfield, Milton Keynes, MK11 3LW, UK
UKHW040225290926
15471UKWH00001B/1